Quilting with Curves

20 GEOMETRIC PROJECTS

Daisy Aschehoug

stashBOOKS.
an imprint of C&T Publishing

Library of Congress Cataloging-in-Publication Data

Names: Aschehoug, Daisy, author.
Title: Quilting with curves : 20 geometric projects / Daisy Aschehoug.
Description: Lafayette, CA : Stash Books, an imprint of C&T Publishing, Inc., [2023] | Summary: "Explore the exciting possibilities that come with sewing curves in your patchwork projects. This selection of 20 beautiful projects includes curved patchwork techniques, from basic to complex. This book is essential for anyone wishing to experiment with both curved piecing and modern quilt design"-- Provided by publisher.
Identifiers: LCCN 2022052606 | ISBN 9781644033678 (trade paperback) | ISBN 9781644033685 (ebook)
Subjects: LCSH: Patchwork--Patterns. | Quilting--Patterns. | Seams (Sewing) | Geometry in art.
Classification: LCC TT835 .A817 2023 | DDC 746.46--dc23/eng/20221114
LC record available at https://lccn.loc.gov/2022052606

Printed in China

10 9 8 7 6 5 4 3 2 1

DEDICATION

For my husband, Erik. Whenever I question whether to try something new, he helpfully reminds me, "It can't be that hard. People do it every day."

ACKNOWLEDGEMENTS

I'd like to thank my family, particularly my mother. She taught me to thread a sewing machine and lent me her old Bernina when I first started sewing. She helped me make my first quilt in 2009. She took me to my first quilting retreat, which was a Mary Lou Wideman event in 2010. And she took me to my first quilt show in Austin, Texas, in 2013. She always said yes when I raided her fabric stash, and her generosity paved my path in quilting. I am forever grateful.

Because my father faithfully accompanies my mother to all the quilting shows, he has been at almost every big event where I have taught or lectured, and those quiet moments sitting with him between workshops or before lectures always calmed my nerves and bolstered my confidence. His support for my business and my art means the world to me.

All of the magazine editors I have worked with have shaped my growth as a designer, and I owe them so much. They helped me refine my style and kept me producing even when my tendency to procrastinate threatened to stall my productivity: Vivika DeNegre (*Modern Patchwork* and *QuiltCon Magazine*), who published my first projects in 2016 and many more after those; Laurie Baker (*Modern Quilts Unlimited*); Alice Hadley and Lorna Slessor (*Love Patchwork and Quilting*); Anna-Karina Caudevilla (*Simply Moderne*); and Wenche Wolff Hatling and Marie Eivik (*Quiltemagasinet*).

And thanks, of course, to Madison Moore, who has provided a steady, guiding hand on this book.

Several manufacturers in the quilting industry generously provided materials and tools to make the quilts in this book. A big thank you to Robert Kaufman Fabrics, Oakshott Fabrics, Studio E Fabrics, Flatter, Olfa, and Aurifil.

So many quilters have influenced my journey that it will be impossible to include everyone. To name a few: Sherri Lynn Wood, Kaffe Fassett, Alexis Deise, Erick Wolfmeyer, Carson Converse, and Jen Carlton Bailly have all directly influenced my quilt designs or my use of the quarter circle square. I'm particularly thankful for the time and effort that Alyssa Haight Carlton, Elizabeth Dackson, Heather Grant, and Jacquie Gering put into the early days of the Modern Quilt Guild and QuiltCon because that event offered so much inspiration to me as a quilter and designer. Least famous but most important of all is Jen Hague, my fellow Triangle Modern Quilt Guild member who sewed a mountain of Drunkard's Path blocks at a sewing retreat sometime in 2014; watching her fly through those blocks led me to a love of curved piecing that has yet to grow old or lose its wonder.

And finally, thanks to my husband, Erik, to whom this book is dedicated. He has gone above and beyond our marital promise to love and support one another. He pushes me to dream bigger and reach higher, and then he creates the space I need so I can work hard to get there. He also makes an amazing chicken fried rice and gets the kids to bed like it's magic. I couldn't ask for a better partner.

CONTENTS

Introduction

Most of the quilts I've made are built with quarter circle squares. Sometimes there are hundreds in a single quilt. Even though I'm drawn to and admire almost all kinds of quilts, there's no question that I'm called to the quarter circle the way I imagine athletes and musicians are drawn to their positions in their fields. I look at the quarter circle square the way builders might look at bricks or the way my children look at Legos—these fun building blocks can be moved and turned and resized and recolored in a variety of ways that all end up constructing something beautiful. Each quilt in this book uses this shape, and my hope is that the diversity of designs show the potential of a single element repeated throughout a composition.

All of the quilts in this book have been previously published in magazines, and all of those magazines, except one, publish modern projects. I find this amusing since I don't consider myself to be a modern quilt designer; I have a deep love and appreciation for traditional quilts as well as art quilts. My quilt designs reflect this range. Some tend toward the modern traditional genre, and a few might pass as art quilts. I think what might make them appeal to modern quilters is the fabric selection—I prefer bright, bold colors.

Some quilts have limited palettes like *Fortune* (page 33) and *Stacked Curves* (page 41), and some quilts include a broader range of colors like *Wired* (page 28) and *Plaid Punch* (page 45). The degree of piecing ranges from quick, minimal designs like *Pivot* (page 86) and *Scoop* (page 37) to the more arduous piecing in *Ginkgo Fans* (page 101) and *Spinning Tradition* (page 118). Several quilts include a range of quarter circle square sizes like *Peppermint Twist* (page 90) and *Halfspots* (page 96). There's even a little improv woven into the instructions for *Midnight Sun* (page 66).

Despite all this variety, one element remains constant: the curve of the quarter circle square. Because that element is in almost everything I've made, I have sewn thousands of these units, and I continue to develop ways to increase my efficiency and accuracy. I've tried to forget the curve and design purely with lines and angles, but those quilts rarely get made. Even though the French philosopher Gaston Bachelard was referring to architecture and physical spaces, his quote about curves resonates with my perspective on quilt design: "The grace of the curve is an invitation to remain. We cannot break away from it without hoping to return." I hope, dear reader, that you return to this book again and again, and find a love for curved piecing that is satisfying.

Choosing Fabrics

FABRIC SUBSTRATES

The first time I sewed curves, I used Peppered Cottons from Studio E Fabrics. Like all shot cottons, the fabric uses a different color on the warp and weft to create a gorgeous depth of color. Not all shot cottons have the same hand, or drape. Some are lighter and more suited for apparel. Others are heavier or thicker. I find that the heavy weight of the Peppered Cottons make for particularly nice, precise curves, and I continue to use shot cottons today.

Regular quilting cotton also has a good weight for curved piecing, and I've found that linens—particularly the Robert Kaufman Fabrics Essex Linens—are delightful to work with. Other heavier substrates like chambrays will sew easily as well, but I recommend regular quilting cotton or linens to beginners.

If it's your first time sewing with curves, avoid lightweight materials like lawns and voiles. These fabrics can be slippery and make it difficult to sew accurately without pleats or puckering. Adding starch to these light fabrics may not help because the concave piece in a quarter circle square needs to be flexible in order to fit around the convex piece (see Anatomy of a Curve, page 12).

COLOR AND CONTRAST

My use of color in quilts tends to be intuitive. I pick colors based on what I think fits with my vision for the design, and I'm rarely indecisive about the palette for any specific project. But, I can spend hours debating the different prints and solids that fall in a specific color palette. I like to focus on contrast, or the differences between two fabrics.

Fabrics showing contrast in hue and value

Fabrics showing contrast between organic and geometric prints

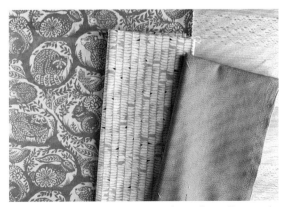

Fabrics showing contrast in size with small, medium, and large scale prints

Contrast in fabrics can mean a distinct difference between the two colors on either side of a seam, like a blue next to a red. It can also mean a difference in value, like a burgundy next to a pink, or a navy next to a pale blue. Contrast also has a variety of meanings when you consider prints: a print next to solid, a large-scale print next to small scale print, geometric prints next to organic/flowery prints, dots next to chevrons, and so on. Many quilt designs in this book benefit from having strong contrasting fabric choices including *Plaid Punch* (page 45), *Sightseeing* (page 51), and *Ladybird Curve* (page 112). Without contrast, these quilts risk looking muddied. The design gets lost if you can't distinguish the piecing lines.

Limiting contrast can also be a useful strategy. *Stacked Curves* (page 41) includes a narrow range of reds from a deep red-orange to a cool, purple-burgundy. *Ginkgo Fans* (page 101) creates the fan shapes by mixing four different prints and solids that all read as the same color. *Scoop* (page 37) and *Vining* (page 60) both offer an ombre effect with subtle transitions of white to gray.

Your fabric choices will have a huge impact on the look of your quilt; make sure to carefully consider my color notes on each project, and give your choices a lot of thought before you make your fabric purchases or use favorite fabrics from your stash.

MAKE DO

Textile manufacturing isn't always environmentally friendly. The process of growing cotton uses tremendous amounts of resources, including water and pesticides. The dyeing process creates byproducts that damage natural ecosystems. Transporting materials from where they are grown to where they are manufactured, and again to where they are sold, requires significant amounts of fuel. I regularly look at my stash of fabric and debate the environmental cost of having such a large collection of material. Some of my quilts were built with the intention of using up my stash.

I'm drawn to navy blues and pinks, and *Ginkgo Fans* (page 101) was intentionally created to use a variety of prints in a tricolor quilt. The project calls for yardage of the three colors, but my hope is that quilters will mix and match the fabrics they already have on hand. The black stripes in *Sirkel* (page 77) are pieced from a mix of treasured scraps and favorite trimmings from the now-closed textile house Umbrella Prints.

Photo by Barbora Kurcova

Even if the design of a quilt isn't suited to a variety of prints, or if your vision for a project doesn't include a variety of prints, I encourage you to incorporate a make-do approach in other ways. If a background material calls for a single color like white, use a range of whites from the beginning so you don't need to purchase more should you run out of material. You might find that even if you don't have yardage of one white from one manufacturer, you likely have a variety of whites or white-on-white prints that can be mixed together. The subtle shifts will add interest to what would have otherwise been a solid background. I ran out of the background material in *Spinning Tradition* (page 118), and I couldn't get more before my deadline for this book. Instead of panicking, I pieced together leftover rectangles so that I would have fabric scraps big enough to create the concave 12″ pieces. If you look very closely, you can see the extra seams, but since the background reads as one entity from a distance, those seams disappear. Buying more fabric wasn't necessary.

DIRECTIONAL FABRICS

The most efficient methods for cutting material (page 14) may not fit with directional prints. Avoid cutting template pieces on the fold or cutting through two layers of material whenever directional prints are used in a project. Before making any cuts with your rotary cutter, double-check the orientation of the template, the direction of the fabric that you are cutting, and the direction of the neighboring fabrics in the project. Using a directional fabric can enhance a quilt design, but do allow for extra material in case of mistakes. It's also more than okay if the directionality is oriented differently throughout the quilt.

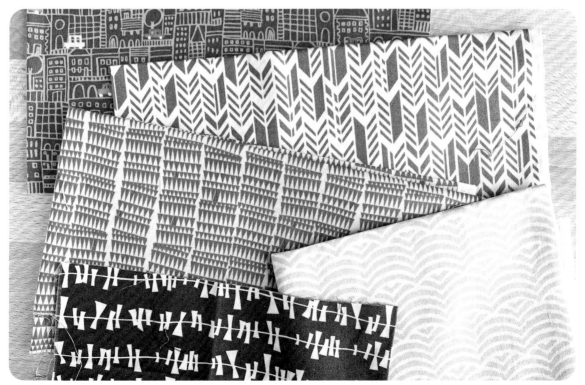

These fabrics have a noticeable direction to them. The motif continues on the x or y axis. When cut and sewn back together, it may look better if the motif continues across the seam.

My Favorite Tools

As a general rule, I take a less-is-more approach to supplies in my studio. I'm not a gadget person, and my main sewing machine only does a straight stitch. I use a simple ¼″ presser foot for my piecing instead of one that's designed for sewing curves.

ROTARY CUTTERS

Larger-diameter rotary cutters (45mm and 60mm) are ideal for cutting long strips or squaring up blocks with a square ruler. Smaller-diameter rotary cutters (28mm and 18mm) are best for cutting small curves, especially the concave curve of the 3″ or 1½″ quarter circle squares. If you are using acrylic templates, the plastic piece in the center of the blade of the 18mm rotary cutter might not clear the height of the acrylic template. Use the 28mm to ensure the blade travels next to the acrylic template for accurate cutting.

RULERS

A straight ruler 24″ long is preferred for cutting strips and large rectangles.

All quarter circle square blocks benefit from trimming. The concave template piece is oversized to allow for both sewing and pressing, and up to ¼″ will need to be removed from the straight edges of that template piece once it is sewn. Square rulers that match the quarter circle square unit size are best (3½″ square ruler for quarter circle squares that finish at 3″ in a quilt, 6½″ for those that finish at 6″, etc.).

PINS

Pins are helpful for basting curves and joining quarter circle square units as you construct the quilt top.

GLUE STICK

There are a variety of textile glues on the market to baste your material before sewing. Anything labeled "permanent" should be avoided. Liquid glue is also not ideal since the glue should be sticky enough to hold two pieces of fabric together with just a second or two of pressure from fingers. I don't use an iron to set the glue before I go to the sewing machine. I find that Roxanne Glue-Baste-It is perfect for appliqué and binding but not good for basting curves. Large diameter Elmer's school glue sticks are acceptable because they are water soluble and sticky, but the glue is challenging to apply in thin lines because of the large diameter.

The best glue sticks are small diameter glue pens. Sewline, Fons & Porter, and Quilters Select all offer these pens. I've used both Sewline and Fons & Porter, and I have found that the refills for both brands work in the other brand's pens. There are a variety of glue types. I have used pink, blue, and yellow and have found that they all work well for sewing quarter circle squares.

Daisy's favorite tools

Cutting tools

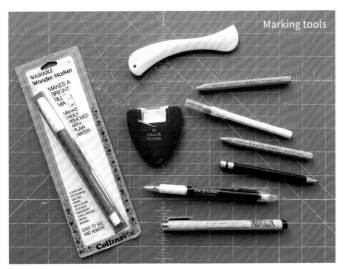
Marking tools

Basting tools

IRON

One of my mantras when teaching is "fabric has a memory." Whenever we stretch, pull, or distort fabric, it eventually finds its way back into the original shape. For that reason, I hold my fabric gently as I press and prefer to use a dry iron. If I have stubborn creases, I will use water from a spray bottle to create some steam. Occasionally, I find that a bit of starch or Flatter smoothing spray is helpful before squaring up blocks, but I never use either of those before cutting and sewing fabric.

Anatomy of a Curve

Whenever you sew a straight seam, the edges of the two pieces of fabric are identical. They line up exactly. This isn't the case with a curved seam, and particularly with curves that are precise or that are intended to match a specific geometric shape. A curved seam always has two shapes that come together to create the seam: a convex shape and a concave shape. The convex shape A is like the curve on the exterior of a round shape (picture the outside of a bowl), while the concave shape B is like the curve on the interior of a round shape (picture the inside of a bowl).

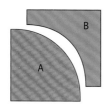

Two pieces of fabric that create a curved seam

The edges of shapes A and B are not identical. This can be seen when attempting to nest the convex template inside the concave template—they do not fit precisely unless overlapped. In order to understand how those two edges differ, it's helpful to look at the radius of the curves that make up each shape.

In the convex shape of a 6″ quarter circle square, the radius, or the distance between the center of a circle and any point on the edge, is 6½″. In the concave shape, we have to look at the negative space of the shape in order to measure the radius. That curve has a 6″ radius.

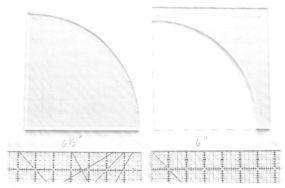

The curves of 6″ Template A and B tools

All quarter circle squares are made up of two curves that differ by ½″. The 3″ quarter circle square uses a 3½″ convex curve and a 3″ concave curve. A 12″ quarter circle square uses a 12½″ convex curve and a 12″ concave curve.

If you forget which is bigger, think about walking past a cave in the woods. In order to block the opening of the cave with a rock, you must find a rock bigger than the mouth of the cave. In this metaphor, our convex piece is the rock, and the concave piece is the cave.

The templates included in this book already do the math for you, but being able to visualize how these two shapes come together will help you with many of the steps in each project. Throughout this book, Template A refers to the convex template piece, and Template B refers to the concave piece. Each curved seam requires an A and a B.

Template B pieces include extra material for several reasons. If Template B were exact, the skinny ends would be challenging to pass under the presser foot accurately, even when using a pointed stick to push the fabric. Once sewn, those ends would also be challenging to press without burning fingertips. Finally, a little bit of extra material makes it easier to trim to an accurate size.

All the required templates appear at the end of this book (pages 124–128). If you prefer, you can also access them digitally by scanning this QR code or visiting the web address below to download the templates.

tinyurl.com/11544-patterns-download

Cutting with Templates

Throughout the book, I use the acronym WOF to mean width of fabric. In general, the most efficient way to cut several quarter circle square template pieces is to do the following:

1. Fold yardage and match the selvedges as shown in the diagram. Most by-the-yard fabric comes with a crease in the desired spot, halfway through the WOF.

2. Cut strips from yardage the width of the pattern pieces.

3. Place the template onto the strip and cut around the templates with a rotary cutter (or trace with chalk or pencil and cut with scissors).

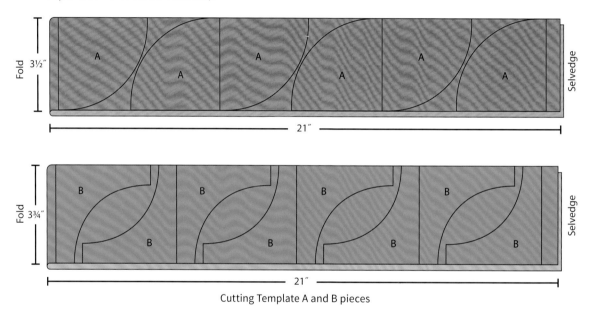

Cutting Template A and B pieces

CUTTING ARCS WITH TEMPLATES

Arcs are formed when there is more than one curve in a quarter circle square unit. I often call these *nested curves*, but they are also referred to as Double Drunkard's Path blocks.

To make an arc, cut a square that is ½″ larger than the largest curve in the block. If the block contains a 3″ and a 6″ curve, then the square needs to be 6½″. Align the right angle of the 6″ convex template with the right angle of the square and trim the corner.

Align the 3″ concave template so the small, flat edges of the template match the remaining straight edges of the square that has been trimmed. Trim the corner.

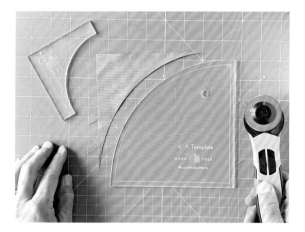
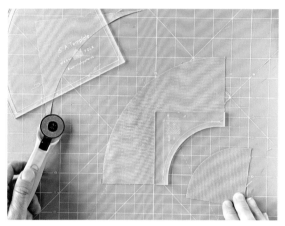

Most quilting fabric is made with thread that runs horizontally and vertically. Cutting along these planes is often referred to as "straight of grain" and leaves a stronger edge to the fabric. Cutting diagonally is called "on the bias" and allows for a bit of stretch, which is usually not desirable in quilt blocks when sewing for accuracy. This approach to creating arcs maintains the straight of grain at the edge of the resulting quarter circle square blocks, but it requires more fabric.

If the goal is to conserve fabric, use the method described above with a piece of poster board or cardstock to make your own template for an arc. Then, place the arc on your fabric as efficiently as possible and make your cuts regardless of where the bias is. Be careful with your blocks after you sew them so they don't stretch or warp before they are sewn into the quilt top.

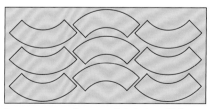
Arrangement of arcs on fabric for efficiency

Basting Template Pieces

NO BASTE

I sewed my very first Drunkard's Path blocks without any pinning or gluing. Many Drunkard's Path templates create a curve that is slightly less than a full quarter circle. The curve is not as steep as a quarter circle, and that small difference makes it a little easier to accurately sew this seam without pins. The quarter circle is just a bit tighter and benefits from some kind of basting. But if you want to give it a try, place the convex piece down first with the right side up. Place the concave piece right side down. Slowly begin to sew, aligning the edges of the fabric as it moves under the presser foot.

GLUE BASTE

To baste with glue, mark the centers of each curve by folding the fabric in half and finger-pressing a crease.

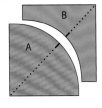

If you are making several quarter circle squares at once, mark the crease with a pencil or chalk. Place the concave piece on top of the convex unit, right sides together. Line up the center creases.

Use a ¼˝ glue stick/pen. Start at the center and apply a small line of glue on the convex piece.

Press Template B piece into the glue, starting at the center and working toward the edge.

Apply another small line of glue, starting at the center and working toward the opposite edge. Finish attaching the Template B piece.

PIN BASTE

To baste with pins, mark the centers of each curve and align the centers as described in Glue Baste. Place a pin in the center creases. Place pins at either end. Fill in between with pins.

The minimum number of suggested pins is three, which includes one at the middle and one at either end. Beginners may find it easier to use many pins or to glue baste.

Sewing, Pressing, and Trimming

SEWING

One of the key elements in sewing accurate curved seams is to use a scant ¼˝ seam allowance. Curved seams do not open the same way that straight seams do, and a scant seam allowance compensates for the difference.

There are several ways to achieve a scant seam allowance. On some machines, the position of the needle can be moved to the left or the right. If the needle position can't be changed, move the fabric to the left and use scraps to test the seam. A scant ¼˝ is just a few threads smaller than the ¼˝ on your ruler, but it is not as small as ⅛˝.

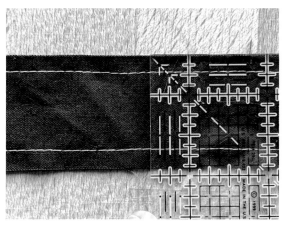

I'm regularly asked if I use one of the presser feet specially designed for curved piecing. I do not. I find that I prefer to see where the fabric passes under the presser foot, and anything with a guide or guard on it blocks my view. I used to sew with a ¼˝ guide, but I found that the movement of material into the presser foot resulted in a generous ¼˝ seam allowance instead of a scant one, which was problematic. The bigger the seam allowance, the smaller the block. There is extra material built into the concave template piece,

but the convex template piece is exact; a large seam allowance results in a convex piece that is too small.

If the sewing machine has a knee lift or a presser foot lift in the foot pedal, this may be the time to get acquainted with that feature. Sometimes fabric pillows up next to the presser foot, and regularly raising the foot to smooth the fabric is helpful.

There is no need to rush these stitches, especially at the beginning. The slowest sewing is required when there is no basting. Pin basting allows for faster sewing, and glue basting usually allows for the fastest stitches.

There is no need to change the stitch length on your machine. Whatever stitch length is used for straight seams is good for curved seams.

PRESSING

Pressing seams toward the center of the circle may create the effect of a raised circle, almost like a button. The opposite is also true: Pressing seams away from the center subtly lowers the circle or creates a slight depression. These effects are most common in smaller circles, and I find that after quilting, they are hardly noticeable. But if they are something that you notice and you have a preference, go for it! Choose the direction that suits your preference.

My design style places curves directly on the edge of the block so that if two circles are placed next to each other, they will touch. Because the curved seam is so close, I find that pressing toward the center of the circle, or toward the convex shape, keeps the seams from being too bulky. I also glue all my seams so there is no danger of "ghosting" when I press toward the lighter side. Ghosting happens when a dark material is pressed to the lighter side and shows up underneath/through the lighter material.

Even if the seams are pressed toward the center of the circle, some seams will contain bulk as you assemble the quilt top. These bulky seams can still be quilted; they simply require a slower go at the quilting stitches.

Each curve ends at the edge of the block. The point where the two half circles touch would have too much bulk if seams were pressed towards the concave side.

The most common mistake in pressing quarter circle squares is to press the block without opening the seam entirely. To ensure the seam opens completely, place the block right side down on the ironing mat. Using your fingertips, start at one end of the curve, pushing against the seam until it opens. Follow along with the iron as you move along the curve. By pressing on the seam, instead of pulling the fabric apart, the block maintains its shape and is not distorted. The stitches reinforce the seam, so there is less danger of stretching the fabric.

The seam was not entirely open on the front. After ironing, there is a slight pocket effect.

If you pull on the fabric, the seam opens further.

Pressing back of block is the easiest way to press the seam towards the convex shape.

If you have puckers or pleats, unpick the seam just before and after the pleat. Press with the iron to flatten the crease. Resew the section of the seam, being sure to backstitch at the beginning and end of the resewn section to secure the thread.

TRIMMING

As I mentioned, Template B pieces are oversized to allow for trimming down accurately. Trim each quarter circle square so there is ¼″ of Template B fabric on either end of the curve. Each finished curve in a quilt (for example 3″, 6″, or 12″) needs to be trimmed to that size plus ½″. So a 3″ quarter circle square will be trimmed to 3½″, a 6″ will be trimmed to 6½″, and so on.

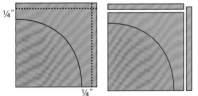

Sewing Quarter Circle Squares

MAKING A HALF CIRCLE

Place quarter circles right sides together and pin and sew on either side of the curved seam.

MAKING A POINT

Pin and sew a straight seam, going through the final stitches of the curved seam for the last ¼″.

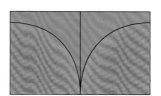

Sewing Strip Slabs (Made Fabric)

Slabs are pieces of "made fabric" that are cut into other shapes to use in quilting. Slabs consist of elements that have been pieced while applying some sort of constraint or rule, such as piecing together one shape again and again. Several projects in this book utilize slabs that consist of strips that are pieced together to resemble striped fabric.

Strip slabs for use inside or outside of curved seams can be tricky, depending on the need for the strips to line up with adjacent quilt blocks. Also, strip slabs have a tendency to shrink relative to the number of seams included in the slab. For example, using 6 strips of 1½″ to make a 6½″ strip slab will likely end up smaller if the seam allowance is at all larger than ¼″. I do a small test with a scant ¼″ seam allowance to see if the slab will end up large enough for the block.

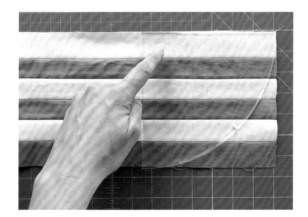 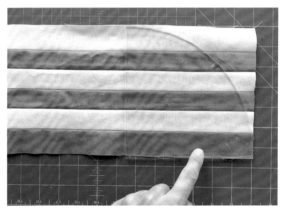

When using strip slabs, orienting the template requires extra attention.

After sewing the strip slab, pay attention to the instructions and the orientation of the template on the strip slab. Check where the straight edges of the template need to align with the strip set. Match the straight edge with either the top or the bottom of the strip set.

Quilt Projects

BLOOMERANG

Finished quilt: 72″ × 72″

The 6″ quarter circle square template set is a good starting point for beginners, and the number of quarter circle square units in this quilt makes for lots of opportunities to practice sewing curves. Alternating pinks and reds create a bit of a floral explosion, and the subtle spin in the petals adds movement to a traditional flower design.

Photo by Øystein Thorvaldsen

Photo by Alva Thylén

Materials

White: 1¾ yards

Blue: 1¾ yards

Pink: 2 yards

Red: 2 yards

Binding: ½ yard

Backing: 4¾ yards

Batting: 80″ × 80″

TEMPLATES

6″ A (convex), page 125

6″ B (concave), page 124

MATERIAL NOTES

- *Essex Linen (E014–308), Essex Blossom (E014–1026), Essex Yarn Dyed Nautical (E064–412), and Essex Wine (E014–1390) from Robert Kaufman Fabrics.*

- *Pieced with 50-weight cotton thread (color 2021) and quilted with Forty3 cotton thread (color 2021) from Aurifil.*

Cutting

White

- Cut 7 strips 6¾″ × WOF. Subcut into 66 Template B pieces.

- Cut 1 strip 6½″ × WOF. Subcut into 1 strip 6½″ × 12½″ and 4 squares 6½″ × 6½″.

Blue

- Cut 7 strips 6¾″ × WOF. Subcut into 66 Template B pieces.

- Cut 1 strip 6½″ × WOF. Subcut into 1 strip 6½″ × 12½″ and 4 squares 6½″ × 6½″.

Pink

- Cut 10 strips 6½″ × WOF. Subcut into 68 Template A pieces.

Red

- Cut 10 strips 6½″ × WOF. Subcut into 68 Template A pieces.

CONSTRUCTION

Creating Quarter Circles

SEAM ALLOWANCE Sew all curved seams with a scant ¼″ seam allowance. Sew all straight seams with an accurate ¼″ seam allowance. Press all straight seams open. Curved seams may be pressed open or toward the center of each circle, toward the Template A (convex) piece. For more, see Sewing, Pressing, and Trimming (page 17).

1. Sew all 6″ Template A pieces to 6″ Template B pieces using the technique in Sewing Quarter Circle Squares (page 20).

Make quarter circle units as shown (Template A/ Template B).

Make 34.

Make 32.

Make 32.

Make 34.

Creating Center Units

2. For Steps 2–4, refer to Fig. 1. Select 2 pink/ white quarter circle squares. Align Template B with the right side of 1 pink/white quarter circle square. Trim. Align Template B with the left side of the second pink/white quarter circle square. Trim.

3. Sew a red Template A piece to the curve of each trimmed pink/white piece. Join the 2 units so the pink curve continues across the 2 blocks.

4. Sew 2 pink/blue quarter circle squares together so the pink forms a half circle. Sew the red/pink/white and pink/blue units together. Set aside.

5. Refer to Fig. 2. Repeat Steps 2–3 with 2 red/blue quarter circle squares to make an inverted version. Repeat Step 4 with 2 red/white quarter circle squares so that the red forms a half circle. Sew the pink/red/blue and red/blue units together. Set aside.

6. Make the remaining units.

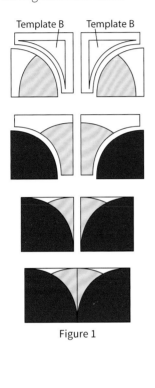

Figure 1

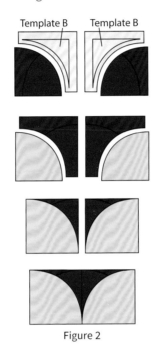

Figure 2

Make 3.

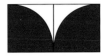

Make 3.

Make 1.

Make 1.

Make the Quadrants

7. Arrange quarter circle squares to make the top left quadrant. Start at the top row of the quadrant and join the units into rows. Join the rows to complete the quadrant.

8. Make another 3 quadrants and 2 center units.

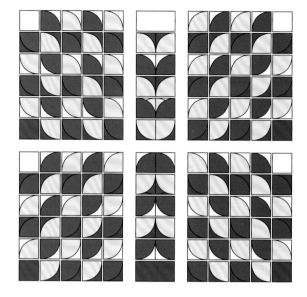

Finish the Quilt Top

9. Join the top and bottom left quadrants, the center units, and the top and bottom right quadrants into 3 columns as shown.

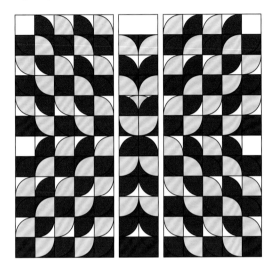

10. Join the columns to finish the quilt top, as shown.

11. Quilt and bind.

Photos by Alva Thylén

WIRED

Finished quilt: 90″ × 90″

Workmen needed to demolish a wall during a kitchen remodel at our house in Baton Rouge. I walked through the worksite midday as they took down the 80-year-old plaster and discovered the old knob and tube wiring left behind after an electrical upgrade. I was fascinated with all the wires coming into the knobs and going back out again—it seemed so dynamic! I reworked my *Spinoff* quilt design into a nine-patch, and I mirrored four of the blocks to make the lines continuous from dot to dot.

Knob and tube wiring

Materials

Fabric A (pink):
1½ yards

Fabric B (dark blue):
2¼ yards

Fabric C (light yellow):
2⅛ yards

Fabric D (light blue):
1⅛ yards

Fabric E (yellow):
1⅜ yards

Fabric F (blue):
1¾ yards

Fabric G (coral):
½ yard

Binding:
⅔ yard

Backing:
8¼ yards

Batting:
98″ × 98″

TEMPLATES

3″ A (convex), page 128

3″ B (concave), page 128

Cutting

Fabric A (pink)

- Cut 3 strips 3¾″ × WOF. Subcut into 36 Template B pieces.
- Cut 9 strips 3½″ × WOF. Subcut into 36 rectangles 3½″ × 9½″.

Fabric B (dark blue)

- Cut 5 strips 3¾″ × WOF. Subcut into 72 Template B pieces.
- Cut 4 strips 3½″ × WOF. Subcut into 36 squares 3½″ × 3½″.
- Cut 12 strips 3½″ × WOF. Subcut into 36 rectangles 3½″ × 12½″.

Fabric C (light yellow)

- Cut 3 strips 3½″ × WOF. Subcut into 36 Template A pieces.
- Cut 5 strips 3¾″ × WOF. Subcut into 72 Template B pieces.
- Cut 4 strips 3½″ × WOF. Subcut into 36 squares 3½″ × 3½″.
- Cut 6 strips 3½″ × WOF. Subcut into 36 rectangles 3½″ × 6½″.

Fabric D (light blue)

- Cut 3 strips 3½″ × WOF. Subcut into 36 Template A pieces.
- Cut 6 strips 3½″ × WOF. Subcut into 36 rectangles 3½″ × 6½″.

Fabric E (yellow)

- Cut 3 strips 3½″ × WOF. Subcut into 36 Template A pieces.
- Cut 9 strips 3½″ × WOF. Subcut into 36 rectangles 3½″ × 9½″.

Fabric F (blue)

- Cut 3 strips 3½″ × WOF. Subcut into 36 Template A pieces.
- Cut 12 strips 3½″ × WOF. Subcut into 36 rectangles 3½″ × 12½″.

Fabric G (coral)

- Cut 3 strips 3½″ × WOF. Subcut into 36 Template A pieces.

CONSTRUCTION

<u>SEAM ALLOWANCE</u> Sew all curved seams with a scant ¼″ seam allowance. Sew all straight seams with an accurate ¼″ seam allowance. Press all straight seams open. Curved seams may be pressed open or toward the center of each circle, toward the Template A (convex) piece.

Sew Quarter-Circle Squares

1. Sew all Template A pieces to Template B pieces using the technique in Sewing Quarter-Circle Squares (page 20). Press and trim.

Make 36.

Make 36.

Make 36.

Make 36.

Make 36.

Make Columns

2. Sew quarter circles to rectangles, and press seams open to make a column 3½″ × 15½″.

Make 20 of each column for the basic quadrants, and 16 of each for the mirrored quadrants.

ORIENTATION OF QUARTER-CIRCLE SQUARES Because the blocks are mirrored, pay attention to the orientation of the quarter circle square when sewing it to a rectangle to make the column.

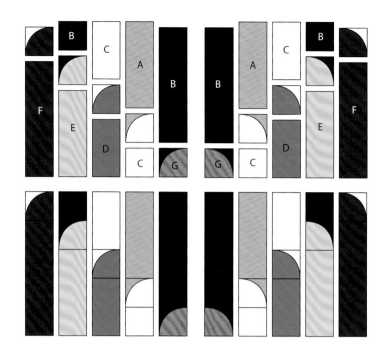

Sew Quadrants

3. Join columns and press seams open to make 20 basic quadrants 15½″ × 15½″ and 16 mirrored quadrants 15½″ × 15½″.

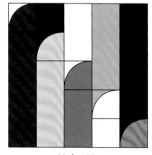
Make 20.

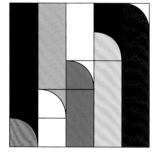
Make 16 (mirrored).

Sew Blocks

4. Join 4 basic quadrants. Carefully match the seams on the center circle, allowing the curve to form a smooth circle shape to make a basic block 30½″ × 30½″. Make 5.

5. Join 4 mirrored quadrants, matching seams to make a basic block 30½″ × 30½″. Make 4.

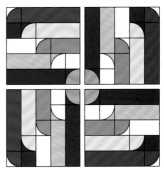

Basic block

Make 5.

Make 4 (mirrored).

Finish Construction

6. Join the 5 basic blocks and 4 mirrored blocks as shown with the mirrored blocks in the center of the top and bottom row.

7. Quilt and bind.

FORTUNE

Finished quilt: 36″ × 48″

Fortune's repeating block is based on the traditional Empire Star quilt block. After substituting quarter circle squares for all the half-square triangles in the original, I saw two shapes that looked like mirrored fortune cookies. The repeat in this design creates a lovely mosaic effect with twists and turns, and repeating circles that emerge where the corners of four blocks come together. The alternating orientation of the block adds a bit to interest to the two-color composition.

Materials

Navy: 1¾ yards

Gray: 1½ yards

Binding (navy): ⅜ yard

Backing: 1¾ yards

Batting: 44″ × 56″

TEMPLATES

3″ A (convex), page 128

3″ B (concave), page 128

<u>MATERIAL NOTES</u>
Nocturnal and Light Gray Pure Solids from Art Gallery Fabrics.

Cutting

Navy

- Cut 16 strips at 3½″ × WOF. Subcut into 192 Template A pieces.

Gray

- Cut 12 strips at 3¾″ × WOF. Subcut into 192 Template B pieces.

CONSTRUCTION

__SEAM ALLOWANCE__ Sew all curved seams with a scant ¼″ seam allowance. Sew all straight seams with an accurate ¼″ seam allowance. Press all straight seams open. Curved seams may be pressed open or toward the center of each circle, toward the Template A (convex) piece.

Quarter-Circle Squares

1. Sew all Template A pieces to Template B pieces using the technique in Sewing Quarter-Circle Squares (page 20).

2. Press and trim 192 quarter circle squares.

Make 192.

Construct Blocks

3. Each block is made with 16 navy/gray 3½″ quarter circle squares. Join 2 navy/gray quarter circle squares to make a 3½″ × 6½″ unit. Make 6 half circles per block for a total of 72 units.

Make 72.

4. Arrange 4 navy/gray quarter circle squares and 6 units from Steps 3 into 4 rows as shown below. Sew squares and units into rows. Press seams open. Sew rows together to make a 12½″ × 12½″ block. Press all seams open. Make 12.

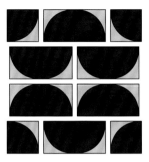 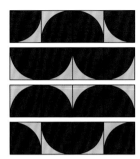 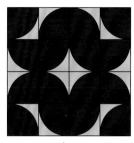

Make 12.

Arrange the Blocks

5. Join the blocks into 4 rows with 3 blocks each. Rotate the blocks so that each block is 90° different from the adjoining blocks.

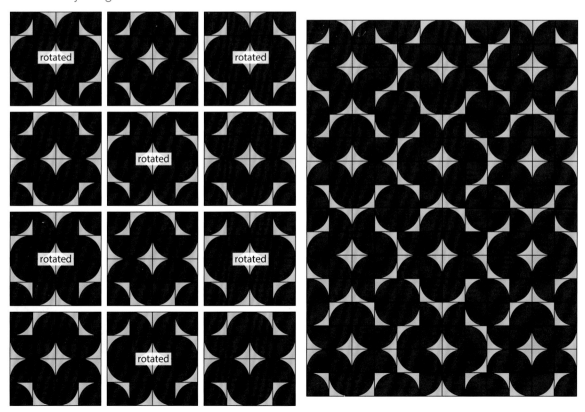

6. Quilt and bind.

Quilting with Curves

SCOOP

Finished quilt: 70″ × 80″

Scoop plays with the idea of foreground and background, just ever so slightly. The placement of colors in an ombre arrangement, and the repetition of the half circles, keeps the viewer's gaze moving inward. The snowy winters in Norway call for regular moments of stillness and inward reflection. The colors for this quilt are inspired by the different shades of white on the landscape and how they interact with the evergreen trees.

Photo by Øystein Thorvaldsen

Materials

Seafoam: 2 yards

Beige: 1½ yards

Ivory: 1½ yards

White: 1 yard

Binding: ⅝ yard

Backing: 5 yards

Batting: 78″ × 88″

TEMPLATES

6″ A (convex), page 125

6″ B (concave), page 124

MATERIAL NOTES

- *Arroyo linen in Seafoam Tics and Stone Treads; Essex linen in Champagne, Ivory, and White from Robert Kaufman Fabrics.*

- *Piecing thread is Aurifil 50-weight cotton (color 2021)*

- *Quilting thread is Aurifil Forty3 cotton (color 2021)*

- *Thread from Aurifil.*

Cutting

Seafoam

- Cut 3 strips 6½″ × WOF. Subcut into 20 Template A pieces.
- Cut 4 strips 10½″ × WOF. Piece for length and subcut into 2 strips 10½″ × 80″.

Beige

- Cut 2 strips 10½″ × WOF. Subcut into 2 strips 10½″ × 36″.
- Cut 1 strip 10½″ × WOF. Subcut into 2 strips 10½″ × 20″.
- Cut 1 strip 6¾″ × WOF. Subcut into 8 Template B pieces.
- Cut 2 strips 4½″ × WOF. Subcut into 4 strips 4½″ × 12½″.

Ivory

- Cut 2 strips 10½″ × WOF. Subcut into 2 strips 10½″ × 36″.
- Cut 1 strip 10½″ × WOF. Subcut into 2 strips 10½″ × 20″.
- Cut 1 strip 6¾″ × WOF. Subcut into 8 Template B pieces.
- Cut 2 strips 4½″ × WOF. Subcut into 4 strips 4½″ × 12½″.

White

- Cut 2 strips 10½″ × WOF. Subcut into 1 strip 10½″ × 36″ and 1 strip 10½″ × 20″.
- Cut 1 strip 6¾″ × WOF. Subcut into 4 Template B pieces and 2 rectangles 4½″ × 12½″.

CONSTRUCTION

SEAM ALLOWANCE Sew all curved seams with a scant ¼″ seam allowance. Sew all straight seams with an accurate ¼″ seam allowance. Press all straight seams open. Curved seams may be pressed open or toward the center of each circle, toward the Template A (convex) piece.

Make Half-Circles

1. Sew all Template A pieces to Template B pieces using the technique in Sewing Quarter-Circle Squares (page 20). Make 4 each of the following quarter circle units (Template A/Template B):

- seafoam/white
- seafoam/beige
- seafoam/ivory

| Make 8. | Make 8. | Make 4. |

2. Join 2 seafoam/ivory quarter circle squares to make a half circle. Make 4 half circle units. Repeat to make 4 seafoam/beige and 2 seafoam/white half circle units. Then add a 4½″ × ½″ rectangle to each of the 10 half circle units, matching colors.

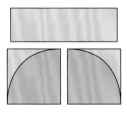

Make 4.

Make 4.   Make 2.

Make Columns

3. Join 2 half circle/rectangle units. Add an ivory 10½″ × 40½″ rectangle to one end of the matching block unit. Join another ivory 10½″ × 20″ rectangle to the other end of the same matching block unit. Make 2. Repeat to make 1 seafoam/white and 2 seafoam/beige columns.

4. Join the columns in ombre order.

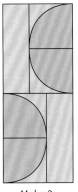
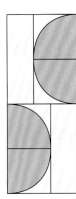
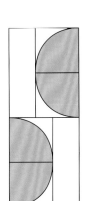

Make 2.   Make 2.   Make 1.

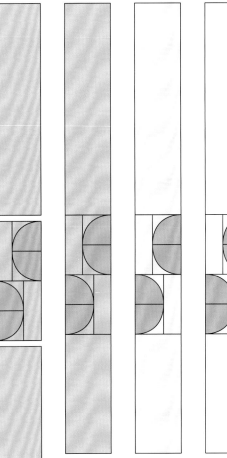

Make 2.   Make 2.   Make 1.

5. Quilt and bind.

STACKED CURVES

Finished table runner: 66″ × 12″

A simple arrangement of quarter circle squares creates an exciting path down the center of the table! The linear groupings are perfect for ombre or rainbow effects, and the repetition of curves is good piecing practice.

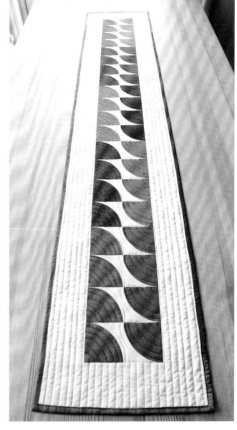

Materials

Red 1: 1 fat eighth

Red 2: 1 fat eighth

Red 3: 1 fat eighth

Red 4: 1 fat eighth

Red 5: 1 fat eighth

Gray: ⅞ yard

Binding: ⅜ yard

Backing: 2⅛ yards

Batting: 20″ × 74″

TEMPLATES

3″ A (convex), page 128

3″ B (concave), page 128

MATERIAL NOTES

- *Assorted Ruby Reds and Gray from Oakshott Fabrics.*

- *Oakshott Fabrics has a 56″ width fabric and this pattern requires a 42″ width fabric.*

- *Pieced with 50-weight cotton thread (color 2021) and quilted with Forty3 cotton thread (colors 2600 and 1103) from Aurifil.*

Cutting

Assorted reds

- Cut 8 Template A pieces from each fat eighth for a total of 40 Template A pieces.

Gray

- Cut 3 strips 3¾″ × WOF. Subcut into 40 Template B pieces.
- Cut 4 strips 3½″ × WOF. Piece for length and subcut into 2 strips 3½″ × 60″ for long borders and 2 strips 3½″ × 12″ for short borders.

CONSTRUCTION

SEAM ALLOWANCE Sew all curved seams with a scant ¼″ seam allowance. Sew all straight seams with an accurate ¼″ seam allowance. Press all straight seams open. Curved seams may be pressed open or toward the center of each circle, toward the Template A (convex) piece.

Quarter-Circle Squares

1. Sew all Template A pieces to Template B pieces using the technique in Sewing Quarter-Circle Squares (page 20).

2. Make 40 red/gray quarter circle squares.

Make 40 (8 of each red).

Make Quarter-Circle Square Units

3. Group 4 quarter circle squares of the same color and sew end to end. Make 2 units from each color for a total of 10 units.

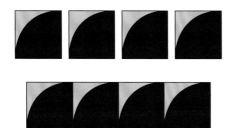

Make 10 (2 of each red).

Make Blocks

4. Sew each quarter circle square unit to a different color unit to make 5 blocks. Mix and match your units in different combinations so the colors appear randomly throughout the project, or create your own pattern with the colors.

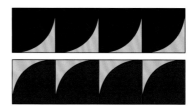

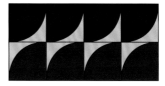

Make 5.

5. Arrange the blocks end to end. Sew the center column of quarter circle squares.

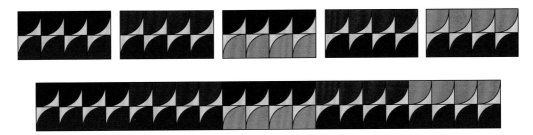

6. Join the long border pieces end to end and add them to the runner. Then add the short border pieces.

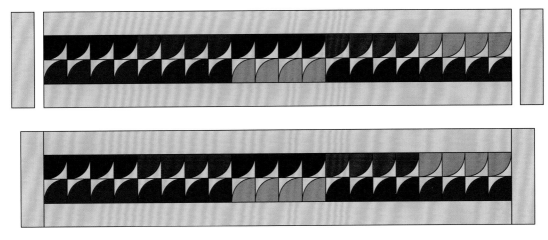

7. Quilt and bind.

PLAID PUNCH

Finished quilt: 78″ × 90″

My favorite Inaluxe art print, from team Kristina Sostarko and Jason Odd, has irregularly curved shapes stacked playfully on each other. I used the palette from the print and tried to create play inside my own usual rules for symmetry and precision. The result is an unexpected plaid with an unpredictable pattern of punched out holes.

Photo by Øystein Thorvaldsen

Materials

Fabric A (pale pink): 1⅞ yards

Fabric B (yellow): ⅝ yard

Fabric C (gold): ⅝ yard

Fabric D (pale blue): ⅔ yard

Fabric E (green): ⅝ yard

Fabric F (dark teal): ⅔ yard

Fabric G (light teal): ⅝ yard

Fabric H (black): ⅔ yard

Fabric I (pomegranate): ⅝ yard

Fabric J (light gray): ⅔ yard

Fabric K (dark gray): ½ yard

Fabric L (dark pink): ⅝ yard

Fabric M (white): ⅔ yard

Fabric N (light green): ⅔ yard

Binding (Fabric F): ¾ yard

Backing: 7¼ yards

Batting: 86″ × 98″

TEMPLATES

3″ A (convex), page 128

3″ B (concave), page 128

MATERIAL NOTES

- *Kona Solids in Canary, Yarrow, Baby Blue, Old Green, Teal Blue, Stratosphere, Pepper, Pomegranate, Ash, Graphite, Blush Pink, White, and Pond from Robert Kaufman Fabrics.*

- *Thread from Aurifil.*

Plaid Punch

Cutting

Fabric A (pale pink)

- Cut 9 strips 6½″ × WOF. Subcut into 52 squares 6½″ × 6½″ and 4 Template A pieces.

Fabric B (yellow)

- Cut 1 strip 6½″ × WOF. Subcut into 1 strip 6½″ × 24½″ and 2 squares 6½″ × 6½″.
- Cut 1 strip 6½″ × WOF. Subcut into 1 strip 6½″ × 18½″, 4 Template A pieces, and 4 Template B pieces.

Fabric C (gold)

- Cut 1 strip 6½″ × WOF. Subcut into 2 strips 6½″ × 18½″.
- Cut 1 strip 6½″ × WOF. Subcut into 3 squares 6½″ × 6½″ and 8 Template B pieces.
- Cut 1 strip 3½″ × WOF. Subcut into 8 Template A pieces.

Fabric D (pale blue)

- Cut 1 strip 6½″ × WOF. Subcut into 2 strips 6½″ × 18½″.
- Cut 1 strip 6½″ × WOF. Subcut into 3 squares 6½″ × 6½″ and 8 Template B pieces.

Fabric E (green)

- Cut 1 strip 6½″ × WOF. Subcut into 3 squares 6½″ × 6½″ and 1 strip 6½″ × 18½″.
- Cut 1 strip 6½″ × WOF. Subcut into 1 strip 6½″ × 36½″.
- Cut 1 strip 3½″ × WOF. Subcut into 12 Template A pieces.

Fabric F (dark teal)

- Cut 1 strip 6½″ × WOF. Subcut into 2 strips 6½″ × 18½″.
- Cut 1 strip 6½″ × WOF. Subcut into 3 squares 6½″ × 6½″ and a rectangle 6½″ × 12½″.
- Cut 1 strip 3¾″ × WOF. Subcut into 4 Template A pieces and 8 Template B pieces.

Fabric G (light teal)

- Cut 1 strip 6½″ × WOF. Subcut into 6 squares 6½″ × 6½″.
- Cut 1 strip 6½″ × WOF. Subcut into 1 strip 6½″ × 18½″.

Fabric H (black)

- Cut 1 strip 6½″ × WOF. Subcut into 6 squares 6½″ × 6½″.
- Cut 1 strip 6½″ × WOF. Subcut into 1 strip 6½″ × 18½″ and 8 Template B pieces.
- Cut 1 strip 3½″ × WOF. Subcut into 4 Template A pieces.

Fabric I (pomegranate)

- Cut 1 strip 6½″ × WOF. Subcut into 6 squares 6½″ × 6½″.
- Cut 1 strip 6½″ × WOF. Subcut into 1 strip 6½″ × 18½″, 4 Template A pieces, and 4 Template B pieces.

Fabric J (light gray)

- Cut 1 strip 6½″ × WOF. Subcut into 1 strip 6½″ × 36½″.
- Cut 1 strip 6½″ × WOF. Subcut into 1 strip 6½″ × 18½″ and 2 squares 6½″ × 6½″.
- Cut 1 strip 3¾″ × WOF. Subcut into 4 Template A pieces and 4 Template B pieces.

Fabric K (dark gray)

- Cut 1 strip 6½″ × WOF. Subcut into 2 strips 6½″ × 18½″ and 3 squares 6½″ × 6½″.
- Cut 1 strip 3½″ × WOF. Subcut into 4 Template A pieces.

Fabric L (dark pink)

- Cut 1 strip 6½″ × WOF. Subcut into 2 strips 6½″ × 12½″ and 2 squares 6½″ × 6½″.
- Cut 1 strip 6½″ × WOF. Subcut into 2 squares 6½″ × 6½″, 8 Template A pieces, and 4 Template B pieces.

Fabric M (white)

- Cut 1 strip 6½″ × WOF. Subcut into 1 strip 6½″ × 18½″ and 3 squares 6½″ × 6½″.
- Cut 1 strip 6½″ × WOF. Subcut into 1 strip 6½″ × 12½″, a square 6½″ × 6½″, and 8 Template B pieces.
- Cut 1 strip 3½″ × WOF. Subcut into 8 Template A pieces.

Fabric N (light green)

- Cut 1 strip 6½″ × WOF. Subcut into 2 strips 6½″ × 18½″.
- Cut 1 strip 6½″ × WOF. Subcut into 1 strip 6½″ × 12½″.
- Cut 1 strip 3¾″ × WOF. Subcut into 4 Template A pieces and 4 Template B pieces.

CONSTRUCTION

Make Quarter-Circle Squares

1. Sew all Template A pieces to Template B pieces using the technique in Sewing Quarter-Circle Squares (page 20). Make *4 of each* of the following quarter circle units (Template A/Template B):

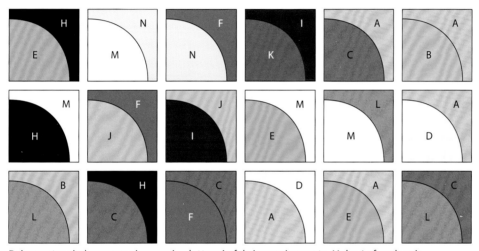

Pair quarter circle square pieces using letters in fabric requirements. Make 4 of each pair.

2. Join 4 matching quarter circle units to form a complete circle. Make 18.

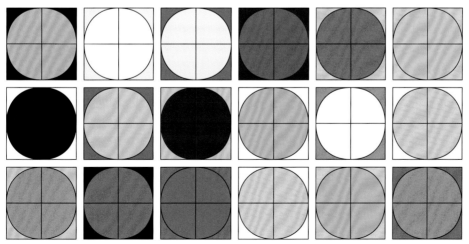

Make 1 of each.

Sew Each Section

3. Follow the section guides for the sewing sequence in each section. Join the sections as shown in the main guide. Press all seams open.

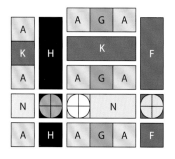
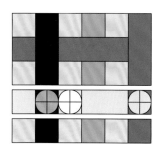
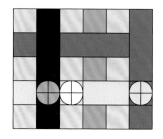

-------- Section A --------

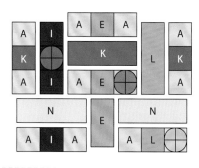
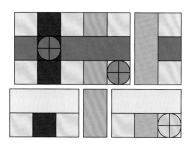
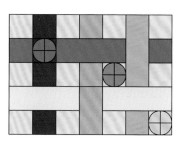

-------- Section B --------

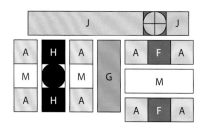
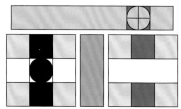
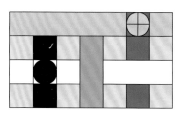

-------- Section C --------

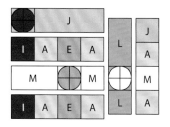
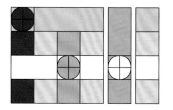
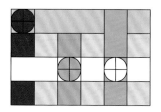

-------- Section D --------

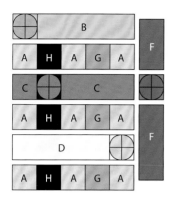
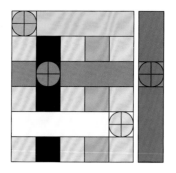
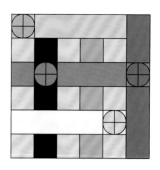

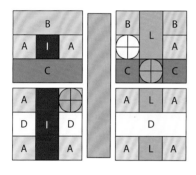
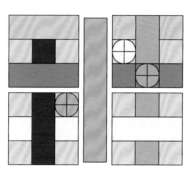
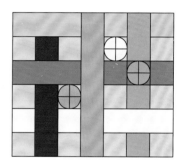

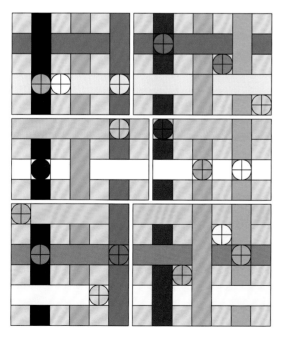
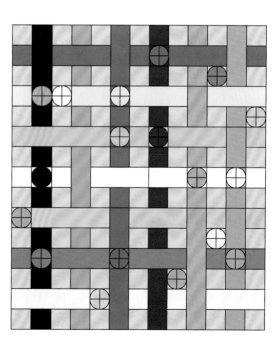

Main Guide

4. Quilt and bind.

SIGHTSEEING

Finished quilt: 64½″ × 86″

Curved piecing adds interest to the large grid in this quilt, and allows for small pops of color throughout. Practice sewing two sizes of curves, 3″ and 6″, with quarter circle templates.

Photo by Øystein Thorvaldsen

Materials

Fabric A (navy): 3¾ yards

Fabric B (white): 2½ yards

Fabric C (red): ¼ yard

Fabric D (pink): ¼ yard

Fabric E (burgundy): ¼ yard

Fabric F (light blue): ¼ yard

Binding: ⅝ yards

Backing: 5¼ yards

Batting: 72″ × 94″

TEMPLATES

3″ A (convex), page 128

3″ B (concave), page 128

6″ A (convex), page 125

6″ B (concave), page 124

MATERIAL NOTES

Kona Solids in Navy, White, Coral, Peach, Ruby, and Cloud from Robert Kaufman Fabrics.

Cutting

Fabric A (navy)

- Cut 4 strips 10″ × WOF. Subcut into 16 squares 10″ × 10″.

- Cut 8 strips 10½″ × WOF. Subcut into 32 squares 10½″ × 10½″. Align the 6″ Template A with a corner of each square to cut 32 Template A pieces.

Fabric B (white)

- Cut 6 strips 3½″ × WOF. Subcut into 24 strips 3½″ × 10″.

- Cut 1 strip 22½″ × WOF. Subcut into 12 strips 3½″ × 22½″.

- Cut 6 strips 6½″ × WOF. Subcut into 32 squares 6½″ × 6½″.

 TIP You will cut 6″ Template B pieces on the opposite side after sewing and trimming the 3″ quarter-circle.

3″ Template A

- Cut 7 from Fabric A (navy) (scraps from the 10½″ squares).

- Cut 5 from Fabric C (red).

- Cut 3 from Fabric D (pink).

- Cut 5 from Fabric E (burgundy).

- Cut 12 from Fabric F (light blue).

CONSTRUCTION

<u>SEAM ALLOWANCE</u> Sew all curved seams with a scant ¼″ seam allowance. Sew all straight seams with an accurate ¼″ seam allowance. Press all straight seams open. Curved seams may be pressed open or toward the center of each circle, toward the Template A (convex) piece.

Make Nested Curve Units

1. Trim a corner of the 6½″ white squares using the 3″ Template B (concave).

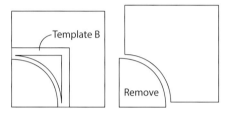

2. Sew all 3″ Template A pieces to the 6½″ Fabric B (white) squares using the technique in Sewing Quarter-Circle Squares (page 20). Make 5 red, 3 pink, 12 light blue, 7 navy, and 5 burgundy squares. Place the unit on your cutting mat and square up so that the color Template A piece is at 3¼″ on either end of the arc.

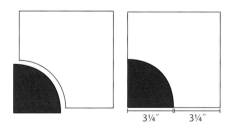

3. Use the 6″ Template A to cut the opposite corner of the Fabric B (white) square. Repeat for all 32 units. Sew Fabric F (light blue) 6″ Template B pieces to Fabric B (white) 6″ Template A white units.

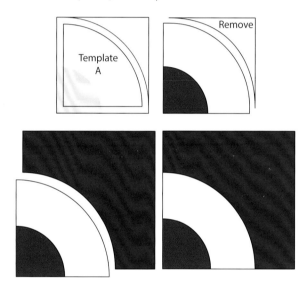

4. Arrange quarter circle units with rectangles. Sew a quarter circle on either side of the 3½″ × 10″ Fabric B (white) strip. Add the 2 quarter circle rows to either side of the 3½″ × 22″ Fabric B (white) strip. Make 8.

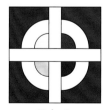

Make 8.

5. Add a Fabric F (light blue) 10″ square to either side of a 3½″ × 10″ Fabric B (white) strip. Sew the units on either side of the 3½″ × 22″ Fabric B (white) strip. Make 4.

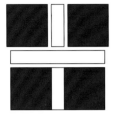 

Make 4.

Photo by Barbora Kurcova

6. Arrange the blocks as shown in the diagram and sew them into 3 vertical rows. Join the rows.

7. Quilt and bind.

Photo by Barbora Kurcova

CURVED DOUBLE STAR

Finished quilt: 54″ × 54″

Curved Double Star utilizes a common traditional quilt block of the same name. Each quarter circle square replaces a half square triangle in the original block design. The secondary patterns that emerge include circles where the edges of the blocks meet as well as a third star where the corners come together.

Photo by Øystein Thorvaldsen

Materials

White: 2 yards

Navy: 1⅛ yards

Berry: 1⅜ yards

Yellow: ⅝ yard

Binding: ½ yard

Backing: 3½ yards

Batting: 62″ × 62″

TEMPLATES

3″ A (convex), page 128

3″ B (concave), page 128

<u>MATERIAL NOTES</u> *Bella Solids in White, Nautical Blue, Boysenberry, and Yellow from Moda.*

Cutting

White

- Cut 12 strips 3½″ × WOF. Subcut into 144 Template A pieces.

- Cut 6 strips 3½″ × WOF. Subcut into 72 squares 3½″ × 3½″.

Navy

- Cut 9 strips 3¾″ × WOF. Subcut into 144 Template B pieces.

Berry

- Cut 5 strips 3¾″ × WOF. Subcut into 72 Template B pieces.

- Cut 6 strips 3½″ × WOF. Subcut into 72 Template A pieces.

Yellow

- Cut 2 strips 6½″ × WOF. Subcut into 9 squares 6½″ × 6½″.

CONSTRUCTION

<u>SEAM ALLOWANCE</u> Sew all curved seams with a scant ¼″ seam allowance. Sew all straight seams with an accurate ¼″ seam allowance. Press all straight seams open. Curved seams may be pressed open or toward the center of each circle, toward the Template A (convex) piece.

Quarter-Circle Square Units

1. Sew all Template A pieces to Template B pieces using the technique in Sewing Quarter-Circle Squares (page 20). Make *72 of each* of the following quarter circle units (Template A/Template B):

- white/navy

- berry/navy

- white/berry

Make 72. Make 72. Make 72.

Make the Blocks

2. Join 2 white/navy quarter circle squares and 2 white squares to make a sub unit. Make 36.

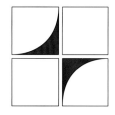 

Make 36.

3. Join 2 berry/navy quarter circle squares and 2 white/berry quarter circle squares to make a sub unit. Make 36.

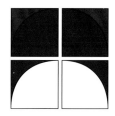 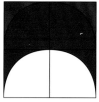

Make 36.

4. Join 4 of each sub unit and a yellow square to make a block. Make 9.

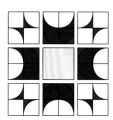 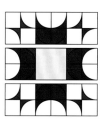

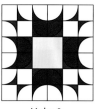

Make 9.

Assemble the Quilt

5. Join the blocks into 3 rows of 3 blocks each.

6. Quilt and bind.

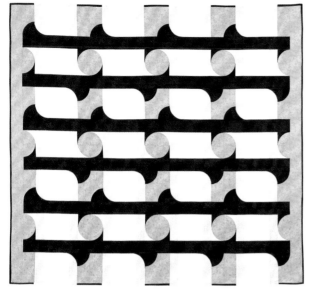

VINING

Finished quilt: 70˝ × 64˝

Reminiscent of the grandeur of Greek architecture, these basic shapes come together to create a mesmerizing vine path around four columns. Playing with ombre prints will enhance the sense of depth in the design.

Photo by Øystein Thorvaldsen

Materials

Navy: 1¾ yards

Pink: 1½ yards

White: ½ yard

Ivory: ½ yard

Cream: ⅞ yard

Gray: 1 yard

Binding (navy): ½ yard

Backing: 4 yards

Batting: 78˝ × 72˝

TEMPLATES

3˝ A (convex), page 128

3˝ B (concave), page 128

MATERIAL NOTES

- *Architextures, Collection CF, and Instead by Carolyn Friedlander, and Kona Solids from Robert Kaufman Fabrics.*

- *Quilted with Forty3 in 2692, 2410, and 2600 thread from Aurifil.*

Cutting

Navy

- Cut 2 strips 3½″ × WOF. Subcut into 24 Template A pieces.
- Cut 3 strips 3¾″ × WOF. Subcut into 48 Template B pieces.
- Cut 10 strips 3½″ × WOF. Piece into one length and subcut into 6 sashing strips 3½″ × 64½″.

Pink

- Cut 4 strips 3½″ × WOF. Subcut into 48 Template A pieces.
- Cut 2 strips 3¾″ × WOF. Subcut into 24 Template B pieces.
- Cut 1 strip 3½″ × WOF. Subcut into 8 rectangles 3½″ × 4½″.
- Cut 2 strips 3½″ × WOF. Subcut 6 rectangles 3½″ × 7½″.
- Cut 4 strips 3½″ × WOF. Piece for length and subcut into 2 side borders 3½″ × 70½″.

White

- Cut 6 strips 2½″ × WOF.

Ivory

- Cut 6 strips 2½″ × WOF.

Cream

- Cut 2 strips 3¾″ × WOF. Subcut into 24 Template B pieces.
- Cut 6 strips 2½″ × WOF.

Gray

- Cut 12 strips 2½″ × WOF.

CONSTRUCTION

SEAM ALLOWANCE Sew all curved seams with a scant ¼″ seam allowance. Sew all straight seams with an accurate ¼″ seam allowance. Press all straight seams open. Curved seams may be pressed open or toward the center of each circle, toward the Template A (convex) piece.

Quarter Circle Squares

1. Sew all Template A pieces to Template B pieces using the technique in Sewing Quarter-Circle Squares (page 20). Make *24 of each* of the following quarter circle units (Template A/Template B):

- navy/pink
- pink/cream
- pink/navy

2. Arrange the navy/pink B quarter circle squares and 3½″ × 4½″ rectangles as shown. Make 24 units; set aside 6 units to use at ends of Rows A and C.

Make 24.

Make 6.

Make 6.

Make 24.

Make 24.

Make 24.

3. Arrange the pink/cream and pink/navy quarter circle squares into circles. Make 24 units; set aside 6 units to use at ends of Row B. Use the remaining 18 units and sew 9 circles.

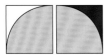 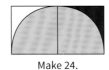

Make 24.

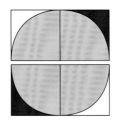 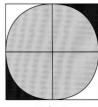

Make 9.

4. Join 2 gray, 1 white, and 2 ivory strips as shown to make a 10½″ × WOF strip set. Make 6.

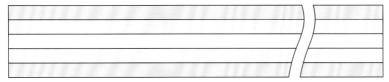

Make 6.

5. Cut the strip sets into 16 units measuring 7½″ × 10½″ and 12 units measuring 6½″ × 10½″.

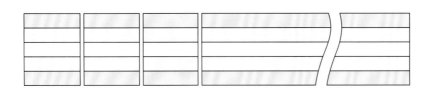

7½″ × 10½″   6½″ × 10½″

Make 16.   Make 12.

 TIP Save strip set leftovers to match the binding up with the patchwork.

6. Place Template A on the lower left and top right corners of a 7½″ × 10½″ strip set unit. Trim the corners. Add a navy Template B piece. Make 8.

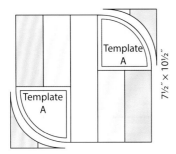  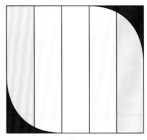

Make 8.

7. Place Template A on the bottom left corner of a 7½″ × 10½″ strip set unit. Trim the corner. Add a navy Template B piece. Make 8.

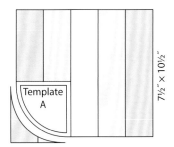
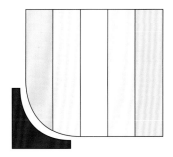
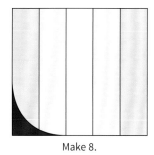

Make 8.

8. Make 2 Row A, 3 Row B, and 2 Row C as shown.

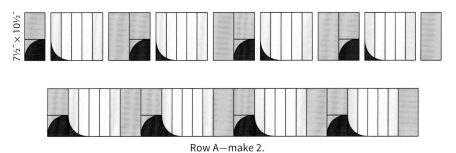

Row A—make 2.

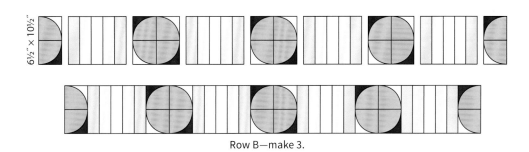

Row B—make 3.

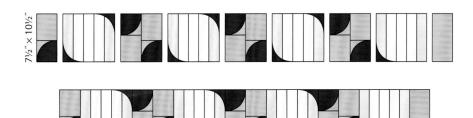

Row C—make 2.

9. Join the rows and 6 sashing strips as shown. Then add the side borders.

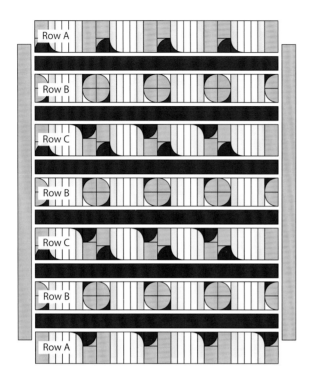

Row A
Row B
Row C
Row B
Row C
Row B
Row A

DIRECTIONAL FABRICS Some of the fabrics are directional in this quilt. To create a sense of order, arrange the blocks so the fabrics flow in the same direction.

10. Quilt and bind.

MIDNIGHT SUN

Finished quilt: 80″ × 80″

This quilt is a perfect place for your favorite scraps. A mix of improvisation and precision creates an arrangement that is unique to each quilter. Instructions include yardage requirements for new fabric, but the steps can be easily adapted to incorporate leftover pieces from other projects.

Photo by Øystein Thorvaldsen

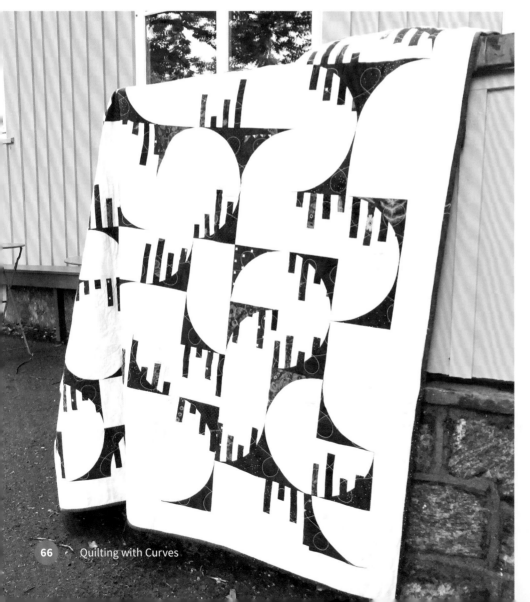

Materials

White: 6⅜ yards

Navy: 4¼ yards

Binding: ⅝ yard

Backing: 7⅜ yards

Batting: 88″ × 88″

TEMPLATES

6″ A (convex), page 125

6″ B (concave), page 124

Cutting

White

- Cut 39 strips 1¼″ × WOF. Subcut 232 strips 1¼″ × 7″.
- Cut 6 strips 6½″ × WOF. Subcut 38 squares 6½″.
- Cut 8 strips 6½″ × WOF. Subcut 48 Template A pieces.
- Cut 1 strip 1″ × WOF.
- Cut 1 strip 2″ × WOF.
- Cut 1 strip 3″ × WOF.

- Cut 1 strip 4″ × WOF.
- Cut 1 strip 5″ × WOF.
- Cut 1 strip 6″ × WOF.
- Cut 1 strip 7″ × WOF.
- Cut 1 strip 8″ × WOF.
- Cut 8 strips 4½″ × WOF for borders. Piece for length and subcut into 2 side borders 4½″ × 80½″ and 2 top/bottom borders 4½″ × 72½″.

Navy

- Cut 16 strips 6¾″ × WOF. Subcut into 96 Template B pieces.
- Cut 1 strip 1″ × WOF.
- Cut 1 strip 2″ × WOF.
- Cut 1 strip 3″ × WOF.
- Cut 1 strip 4″ × WOF.
- Cut 1 strip 5″ × WOF.
- Cut 1 strip 6″ × WOF.
- Cut 1 strip 7″ × WOF.
- Cut 1 strip 8″ × WOF.

CONSTRUCTION

SEAM ALLOWANCE Sew all curved seams with a scant ¼″ seam allowance. Sew all straight seams with an accurate ¼″ seam allowance. Press all straight seams open. Curved seams may be pressed open or toward the center of each circle, toward the Template A (convex) piece.

Strip Set Assembly

1. Match the white and blue WOF strips as shown to make 8 strip sets 8½″ × WOF.

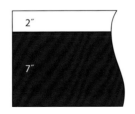

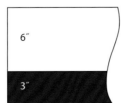

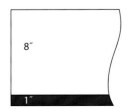

Make 1 of each strip set.

2. Cut each strip unit into 32 strips 1¼″ × 8½″.

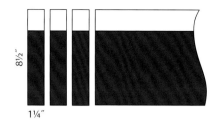

8½″

1¼″

3. Arrange 4 white 1¼″ × 7″ strips and 4 random blue/white strip units together, starting with a white strip on the left and alternating solid and pieced strips. Position all pieced strips with the blues on the bottom. You can slightly adjust the placement of the pieced strips to vary the heights of the blues. Join the strips, press seams open, and trim to a 6½″ square.

 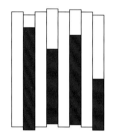  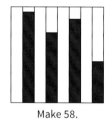

Trim to 6½″ × 6½″.

Make 58.

4. Make 58 strip set squares. Set aside 14 strip set squares.

Quarter Circle Squares

5. Sort the 44 remaining squares into 2 stacks as shown. One stack will be trimmed with the template on the bottom left corner, and the other stack will be trimmed with the template on the bottom right corner. Trim the corner of the block that has the longest blue rectangle. If the corner with a short rectangle is trimmed, all of the blue might get cut away and the investment in piecing that section will be lost.

Stack #1.

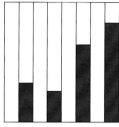

Stack #2.

6. Trim each strip set stack with Template A, aligning the template so the blue ends of the strips are cut away. The 2 stacks should mirror each other, as shown below.

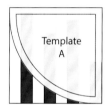

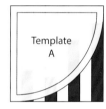

7. Sew the navy Template B pieces to the Template A strip set pieces. Press seams open or toward blue.

Make 22.

Make 22.

8. Sew the navy Template B pieces to the solid white Template A pieces. Press seams open or toward blue. Make 44.

Make 44.

Quilt Assembly

9. Arrange the following blocks improvisationally into 12 rows of 12 blocks on a design board using the following guidelines:

- Orient blue strips vertically.

- No more than 2 similar kinds of blocks should be placed adjacent.

- No group of 4 blocks should make a complete circle.

10. Join the blocks.

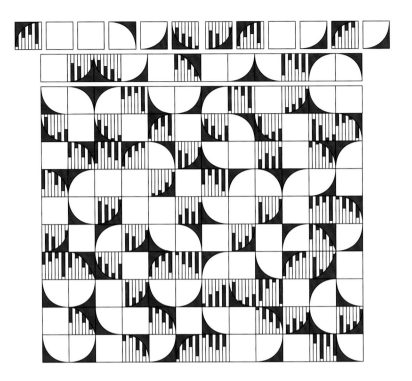

11. Add the side borders. Then add the top and bottom borders.

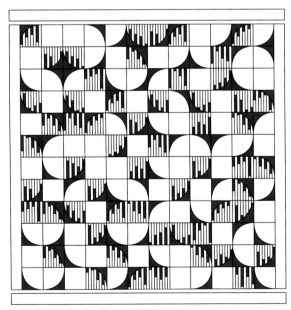

12. Quilt and bind.

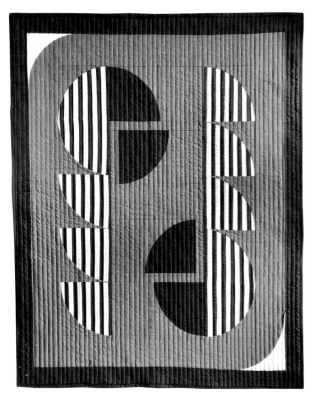

MYSTERY KEYS

Finished quilt: 34″ × 41″

Sometimes I push shapes around like game pieces, and they take on a life of their own. While playing with stripes and curves one day, this key shape appeared. I nestled two of the keys together without much thought about what they'd unlock, but perhaps they will become a bit of art for the wall or a small blanket to entertain a toddler in a pram.

Materials

Blue: 1 yard

White: ⅔ yard

Gold: 1⅛ yards

Binding (blue): ⅓ yard

Backing: 1⅜ yards

Batting: 42″ × 49″

TEMPLATES

6″ A (convex), page 125

6″ B (concave), page 124

<u>MATERIAL NOTES</u> *Navy and White from Oakshott Cottons, and Basics in Freckles by Cotton+Steel for RJR Fabrics.*

Cutting

Blue

- Cut 1 strip 6½″ × WOF. Subcut into 4 Template A pieces.

- Cut 4 strips 2½″ × WOF. Subcut 2 side borders 2½″ × 40″ and 2 top/bottom borders 2½″ × 30″.

- Cut 12 strips 1″ × WOF.

White

- Cut 1 strip 6¾″ × WOF. Subcut into 2 Template B pieces.

- Cut 12 strips 1″ × WOF.

Gold

- Cut 1 strip 6¾″ × WOF. Subcut into 14 Template B pieces.

- Cut 1 strip 6½″ × WOF. Subcut into 2 rectangles 6½″ × 5½″, 2 rectangles 6½″ × 4½″, and 2 strips 6½″ × 1½″.

- Cut 1 strip 4½″ × WOF. Subcut into 2 strips 4½″ × 11½″. Subcut one of the strips into 2 strips 1½″ × 11½″.

- Cut 4 strips 4″ × WOF. Subcut into 2 strips 4″ × 37½″ and 2 strips 4″ × 23½″.

CONSTRUCTION

Sew Strip Sets and Quarter-Circle Squares

1. Join 6 white and 6 blue 1″ × WOF strips into a strip set, alternating white and blue. Make 2.

2. Arrange both strip sets with the blue on the bottom. Cut 10 Template A pieces from the strip sets. Orient 8 of the pieces in the same direction, and mirror the remaining 2. Align a straight edge of the template with the bottom blue strip.

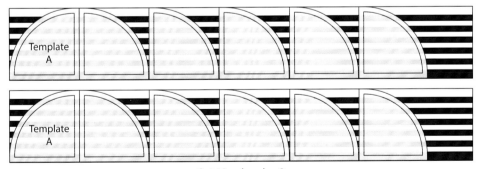

Cut 10, mirroring 2.

3. Add a gold Template B piece to each of the Template A pieces (striped and solid blue), as shown.

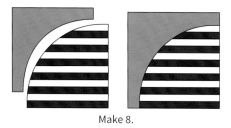

Make 8.

Make 2.

Make 4.

Make the Side Columns

4. Join 5 striped quarter circle squares (1 reversed) into 2 columns as shown into a column. Make 2.

Make 2.

Make the Center Column

5. Add the 5½″ × 6½″ rectangle to a blue/gold quarter circle square as shown.

6½″ × 5½″

6. Add a 4½″ × 6½″ rectangle, and a 1½″ × 6½″ strip to a blue/gold quarter circle square as shown.

6½″ × 1½″   6½″ × 4½″

7. Join the 2 sections to a 1½″ × 11½″ strip as shown. Make 2.

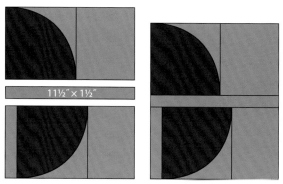

11½″ × 1½″

Make 2.

8. Join both units to a 4½″ × 11½″ rectangle as shown to make the center column.

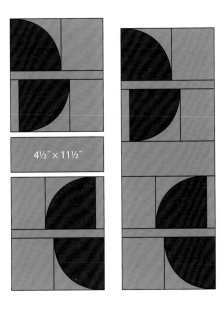

4½″ × 11½″

9. Join the 3 columns as shown.

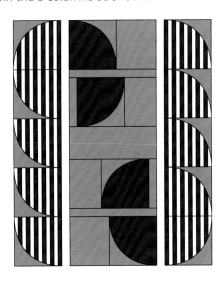

10. Add the 23½″ gold strips to the top and bottom of the quilt. Then add the 4″ × 37½″ gold strips to the sides.

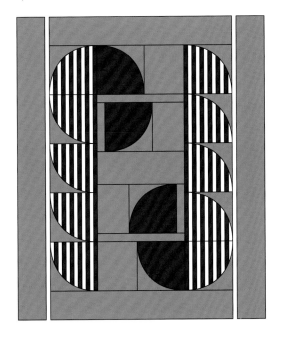

Corners

11. Using Template A on the top left corner, mark the ends of the straight edges of the template. Trim to create a rounded Template A shape.

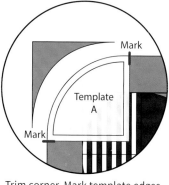

Trim corner. Mark template edges.

12. Fold the rounded corner so the marked points touch to find the center of the curve; mark it. Using all 3 marked points as guides, add the white Template B piece to the rounded corner.

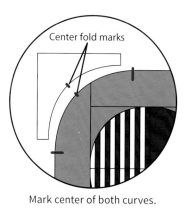

Mark center of both curves.

13. Repeat with the bottom right corner.

14. Add the side borders. Then add the top and bottom borders.

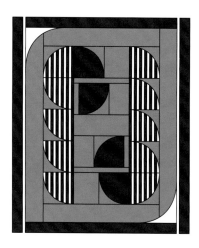

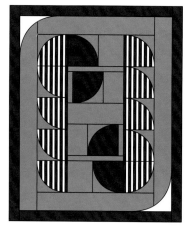

15. Quilt and bind.

SIRKEL

Finished quilt: 68″ × 87″

Inspired by seven-foot-tall metal iron work on the back of an Oslo grocery store, *Sirkel* tests advanced skills in precision piecing and curved seams. Include favorite scraps in the strip piecing to add variation and interest in the composition.

Photo by Øystein Thorvaldsen

Photo by Alva Thylén

Materials

White: 6½ yards

Black: 2¼ yards

Binding: ⅝ yard

Backing: 5⅜ yards

Batting: 76″ × 95″

TEMPLATES

12″ A (convex), pages 124–127

12″ B (concave), pages 124–126

Cutting

White

- Cut 48 strips 1½″ × WOF. Subcut into 144 strips 1½″ × 13″.

- Cut 3 strips 12¾″ × WOF. Subcut into 16 Template B pieces.

- Cut 2 squares 36″. Subcut each square once diagonally into 2 triangles for a total of 4 triangles.

- Cut 4 strips 10″ × WOF. Piece for length and subcut into 2 borders 10″ × 70″.

Black

- Cut 48 strips 1½″ × WOF. Subcut into 144 strips 1½″ × 13″.

CONSTRUCTION

SEAM ALLOWANCE Sew all curved seams with a scant ¼″ seam allowance. Sew all straight seams with an accurate ¼″ seam allowance. Press all straight seams open. Curved seams may be pressed open or toward the center of each circle, toward the Template A (convex) piece.

Strip Slabs and Quarter-Circles

1. Join 9 black and 9 white 1½″ strips to make a 13″ × 18½″ slab. Make 16.

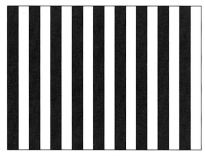

Make 16.

2. Place a Template B on the slab aligning the center line on the arc and the point of the right angle with the center seam of the slab. Note which color is to the left of the seam and which is to the right. Cut 16 template pieces, 8 with black on the left and 8 with white on the left.

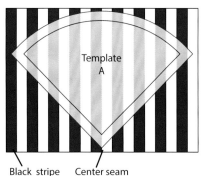

Black stripe   Center seam

Make 8 with black on left. Align template point on center seam.

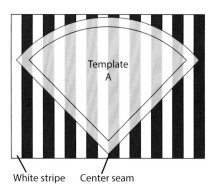

White stripe   Center seam

Make 8 with white on left. Align template point on center seam.

3. Sew Template B pieces to the Template A pieces.

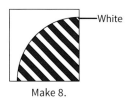

White

Make 8.

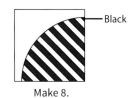

Black

Make 8.

Make Circles

4. Join 4 quarter circles as shown in the illustration to make a full circle, matching the white corners and the black corners. Make 4.

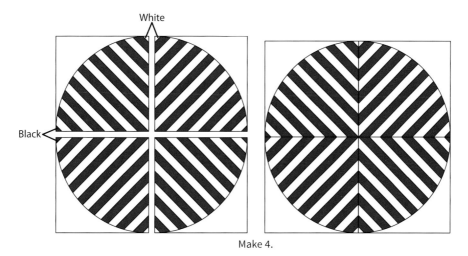

Make 4.

5. Join 4 complete circles, aligning the black squares and the white squares where the circles meet as shown.

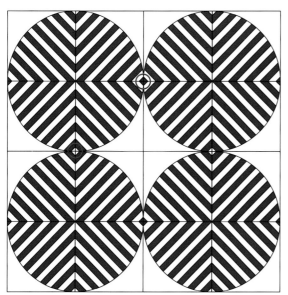

Contact points between circles create black or white squares.

6. Sew the long edge of each white triangle to each side of the square unit.

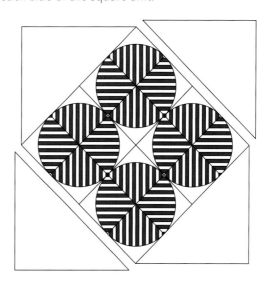

7. Add the borders.

8. Quilt and bind.

BUMPS AND THORNS

Finished quilt: 75″ × 99″

Bumps and Thorns is one of my most personal designs. The arrangement of pink half circles and blue points is a visual autobiography of a specific time in life involving conflicting feelings. The alternating elements of smooth and sharp represent those feelings while creating texture and rhythm in the vertical tracks that run the length of the quilt.

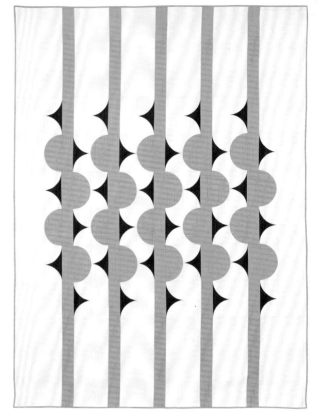

Photo by Øystein Thorvaldsen

Materials

Natural: 5¼ yards

Pink: 2½ yards

Blue: 1¼ yards

Binding: ¾ yards

Backing: 7 yards

Batting: 83″ × 107″

TEMPLATES

4½″ A (convex), page 127

4½″ B (concave), page 127

MATERIAL NOTES *Kona Solids in Natural (1242), Melon (1228), Deep Blue (1541), and Drawn in wideback (AWTX-154451–1) by Angela Walters for Robert Kaufman Fabrics.*

Cutting

Natural

- Cut 6 strips 5¼″ × WOF. Subcut into 60 Template A pieces.

- Cut 4 strips 5″ × WOF. Subcut into 40 Template B pieces.

- Cut 8 strips 9½″ × WOF. Subcut into 8 strips 9½″ × 22½″ and 8 strips 9½″ × 5″.

- Cut 4 strips 12½″ × WOF. Subcut into 2 strips 12½″ × 22½″ and 2 strips 12½″ × 22″.

Pink

- Cut 5 strips 5″ × WOF. Subcut into 40 Template A pieces.

- Cut 13 strips 3½″ × WOF. Piece into one length and subcut into 5 sashing strips 3½″ × 99″.

Blue

- Cut 6 strips 5¼″ × WOF. Subcut into 60 Template B pieces.

Quarter-Circle Squares

1. Sew all Template A pieces to Template B pieces using the technique in Sewing Quarter-Circle Squares (page 20).

Make the following quarter circle units (Template A/Template B):

- 40 pink/natural

- 60 natural/blue

Make 40.

Make 60.

2. Pair 2 blue/natural blocks right sides together to make the "thorns" and sew along the blue edges. Press seams open. Make 30 thorn blocks. Fig 2.

Make 30 blue thorns.

TIP If you see some of the blue in the seams of your "thorns" under the natural fabric, trim the blue fabric in those seams so that it does not show through your background fabric.

3. Pair 2 pink/background blocks right sides together to make the "bumps" and sew along the pink edges. Press seams open. Make 20 bump blocks.

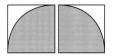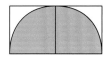

Make 20 pink bumps.

4. Join 3 thorns and 2 bumps as shown to make a strip. Make 10. Set 2 aside.

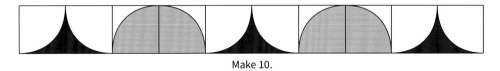

Make 10.

5. Add a 5″ × 9½″ background piece to the end of the strip. Make 8.

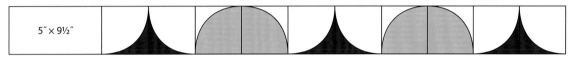

5″ × 9½″

Make 8.

6. Join 2 strips from Step 5 as shown. Then add a 9½″ × 22½″ strip to each end to make an inner column. Press seams open. Make 4.

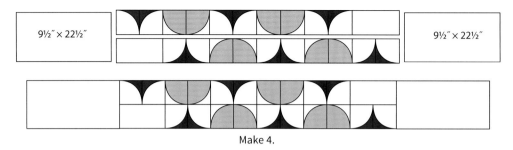

Make 4.

7. Join 2 natural 8″ × 23″ rectangles end to end. Press seams open. Add them to one of the remaining bumps and thorns units. Then add a 12½″ × 22″ strip and a 12½″ × 32½″ strip to either end to make a side column. Make 2.

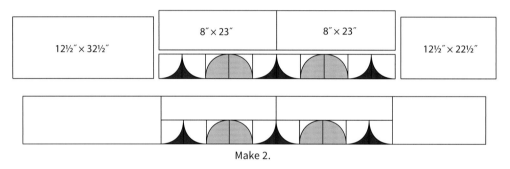

Make 2.

8. Join the 4 inner and 2 side columns as shown with alternating pink 3½″ × 99″ sashing strips.

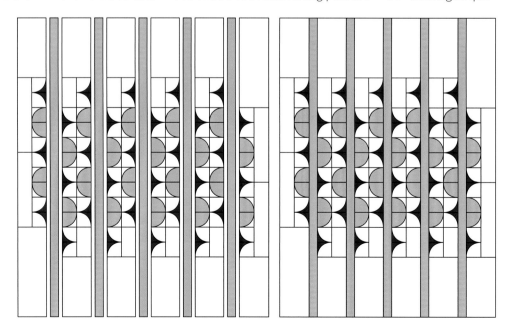

9. Quilt and bind.

Photo by Øystein Thorvaldsen

PIVOT

Finished quilt: 55˝ × 74˝

The flamingo exhibit sits next to our usual snack spot at the zoo. I love the range of pinks in the flamingo feathers and the way they stand so gracefully on one leg. Their physiology is fascinating—from the way they acquire their pigmentation to the way those knobby parts of their legs are actually their ankles, not their knees. Most of the leg is actually a very large foot. *Pivot* uses a flamingo palette and traces some of those long leggy lines from quilt top to bottom.

Photo by Barbora Kurcova

Materials

Pale pink: 3⅝ yards

White: ⅜ yard

Red: 1 fat eighth

Binding: ½ yard

Backing: 3¾ yards

Batting: 63˝ × 82˝

TEMPLATES

1½˝ A (convex), page 128

1½˝ B (concave), page 128

3˝ A (convex), page 128

3˝ B (concave), page 128

<u>MATERIAL NOTES</u> *Assorted Bella Solids from Moda and Basics by Cotton+Steel.*

Cutting

Pale pink

- Cut 3 strips 20½″ × WOF. Subcut into 1 strip 20½″ × 39½″, 1 strip 20½″ × 39″, 1 strip 20½″ × 15½″, and 1 strip 20½″ × 15″.

- Cut 3 strips 12″ × WOF. Subcut into 1 strip 12″ × 28½″, 1 strip 12″ × 27″, 1 strip 12″ × 20½″, 1 strip 12″ × 19″, 1 strip 12″ × 12½″, and 1 strip 12″ × 11″.

- Cut 1 strip 3½″ × WOF. Subcut into 3 squares 3½″ × 3½″ and 3 strips 3½″ × 6½″.

- Cut 1 strip 7½″ × WOF. Subcut into 3 strips 7½″ × 6½″ and 3 strips 7½″ × 4½″.

- Cut 2 strips 3¾″ × WOF. Subcut into 12 Template B 3″ pieces.

White

- Cut 3 strips 2″ × WOF. Subcut into 3 strips 2″ × 7½″, 3 strips 2″ × 9½″, and 3 strips 2″ × 12½″.

- Cut 1 strip 3¾″ × WOF. Subcut into 12 arcs with 1½″ Template A and 3″ Template B. (See Cutting Arcs with Templates, page 15).

Red

- Cut 1 strip 2″ × 20″. Subcut into 12 Template A 1½″ pieces.

CONSTRUCTION

SEAM ALLOWANCE Sew all curved seams with a scant ¼″ seam allowance. Sew all straight seams with an accurate ¼″ seam allowance. Press all straight seams open. Curved seams may be pressed open or toward the center of each circle, toward the Template A (convex) piece.

Sew Square Units

1. Sew all red 1½″ Template A pieces and all pale pink 3″ Template B pieces to white arcs using the technique in Sewing Quarter-Circle Squares (page 20). Make a total of 12 nested curve units.

Make 12.

2. Join 2 nested curve units to make a half circle, matching both of the seams. Make 6 half circle units.

 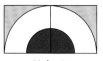

Make 6.

3. Assemble rectangles and nested curve units as shown in Fig. 1 to make a block. Make 3.

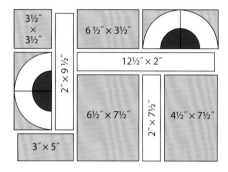

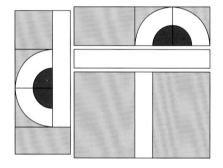 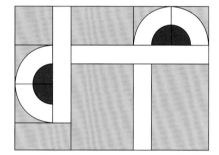

Figure 1. Make 3.

4. Assemble the quilt as shown in Fig. 2.

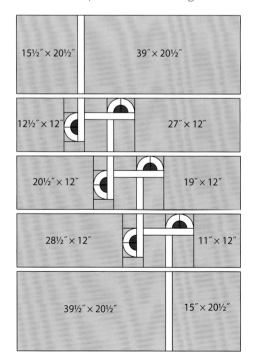 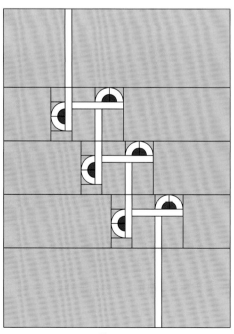

Figure 2

5. Quilt and bind.

PEPPERMINT TWIST

Finished quilt: 63″ × 87″

Who doesn't love the gift of warmth and snuggles? Nested quarter circle squares are easier than they look, and the large blocks are perfect for a quick holiday quilt gift. There are no continuous curves for half or full circles in this design, which means it's perfect for all levels of experience.

Photo by Øystein Thorvaldsen

Materials

Red: ³⁄₈ yard

Light pink: 4¼ yards

Dark pink: 2¾ yards

Binding (red): ⁵⁄₈ yard

Backing: 5½ yards

Batting: 71″ × 95″

TEMPLATES

3″ A (convex), page 128

3″ B (concave), page 128

6″ A (convex), page 125

6″ B (concave), page 124

12″ A (convex), pages 124–127

12″ B (concave), pages 124–126

MATERIAL NOTES

• *Essex linen in Wine, Kona Solids in Pink and Rose from Robert Kaufman Fabrics.*

• *Pieced with 50-weight cotton thread (color 2024) and quilted with Forty3 cotton thread (color 2311) from Aurifil.*

Cutting

Red

- Cut 2 strips 3½″ × WOF. Subcut into 24 Template A 3″ pieces.

Light pink

- Cut 4 strips 12¾″ × WOF. Subcut into 24 Template B 12″ pieces.

- Cut 6 strips 4″ × WOF. Subcut into 24 rectangles 4″ × 3½″ and 24 rectangles 4″ × 6″.

- Cut 2 strips 3¾″ × WOF. Subcut into 24 Template B 3″ pieces.

- Cut 18 strips 3½″ × WOF. Piece 13 strips for length and subcut into 5 vertical sashing strips 3½″ × 81½″ and 2 top/bottom borders 3½″ × 63½″. Subcut the remaining strips into 12 rectangles 3½″ × 12½″.

Dark pink

- Cut 3 strips 6¾″ × WOF. Subcut into 24 Template B 6″ pieces.

- Cut 4 strips 6½″ × WOF. Subcut into 24 rectangles 6½″ × 7″.

- Cut 4 strips 10″ × WOF. Subcut into 24 rectangles 10″ × 6½″.

CONSTRUCTION

SEAM ALLOWANCE Sew all curved seams with a scant ¼″ seam allowance. Sew all straight seams with an accurate ¼″ seam allowance. Press all straight seams open. Curved seams may be pressed open or toward the center of each circle, toward the Template A (convex) piece.

Quarter-Circle Squares

1. Sew all red 3″ Template A pieces to light pink 3″ Template B pieces using the technique in Sewing Quarter-Circle Squares (page 20) to make 24 quarter circle square units of red/light pink.

Make 24.

2. Add light pink 4″ × 3½″ and 4″ × 6″ rectangles to the 3″ quarter circle squares as shown.

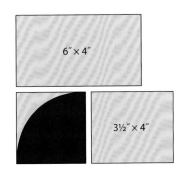

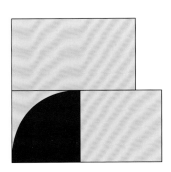

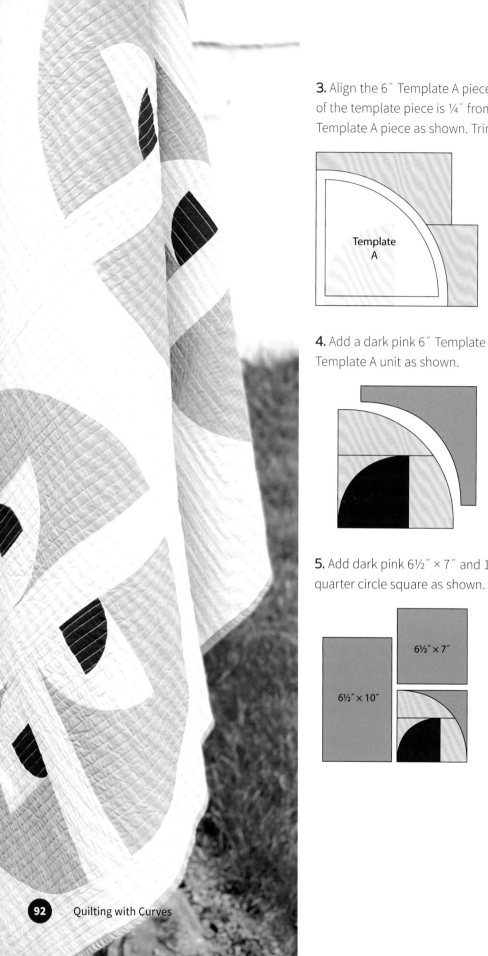

3. Align the 6″ Template A piece so that the right angle of the template piece is ¼″ from the edge of the red 3″ Template A piece as shown. Trim.

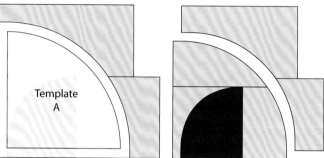

4. Add a dark pink 6″ Template B piece to the trimmed 6″ Template A unit as shown.

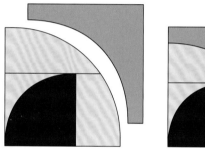
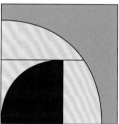

5. Add dark pink 6½″ × 7″ and 10″ × 6½″ rectangles to a 6″ quarter circle square as shown.

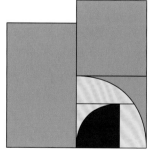

6. Align the 12″ Template A piece so the right angle of the template piece is ¼″ from the edge of the 6″ Template A piece as shown. Trim.

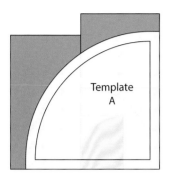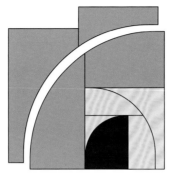

7. Add a light pink 12″ Template B piece to the trimmed 12″ Template A unit as shown. Make 24.

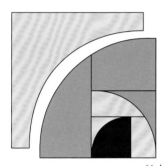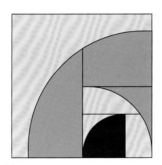

Make 24.

8. Add 2 quarter circle units to a 3½″ × 12½″ rectangles as shown. Make 12.

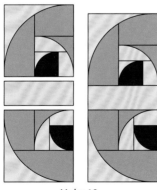

Make 12.

9. Join 3 units, alternating the orientation, to make a 12½″ × 81½″ column. Make 4.

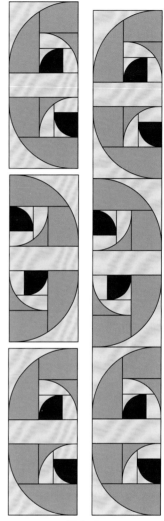

Make 4.

10. Join the 4 columns, alternating the orientation, and 5 vertical 3½″ × 81½″ sashing strips as shown. Then add the top and bottom borders.

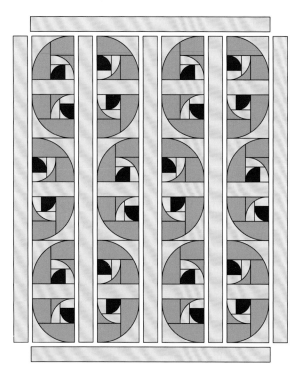

Photo by Alva Thylén

11. Quilt and bind.

Photo by Øystein Thorvaldsen

HALFSPOTS

Finished quilt: 51″ × 80″

This quilt began as a doodle when I was exploring ways to include long lines and a broad range of curve sizes.

Materials

Blue: 3⅜ yards

White: 1⅝ yards

Red: ½ yard

Binding: ½ yard

Backing: 5 yards

Batting: 59″ × 88″

TEMPLATES

1½″ A (convex), page 128

1½″ B (concave), page 128

3″ A (convex), page 128

3″ B (concave), page 128

6″ A (convex), page 125

6″ B (concave), page 124

12″ A (convex), pages 124–127

12″ B (concave), pages 124–126

MATERIAL NOTES *Kona Solids in Lapis, Natural, and Poppy from Robert Kaufman Fabrics.*

Cutting

Blue

- Cut 2 strips 12¾″ × WOF. Subcut into 8 Template B 12″ pieces.

- Cut 1 strip 3¾″ × WOF. Subcut into 10 Template B 3″ pieces.

- Cut 3 strips 11¾″ × WOF. Subcut into 2 strips 11¾″ × 39½″, 1 strip 11¾″ × 27½″, 1 strip 11¾″ × 10½″, and 1 strip 11¾″ × 3½″.

- Cut 1 strip 15½″ × WOF. Subcut into 1 strip 15½″ × 30½″. Subcut remainder to a rectangle 13¼″ × 11½″.

- Cut 1 strip 6½″ × WOF. Subcut into 1 strip 6½″ × 29″.

- Cut 2 strips 8¾″ × WOF. Subcut into 1 strip 8¾″ × 23″ and 1 strip 8¾″ × 23″.

- Cut 1 strip 3½″ × WOF. Subcut into 1 rectangle 3½″ × 11″, 1 rectangle 3½″ × 6½″, 1 rectangle 3½″ × 6, and 2 rectangles 3½″ × 3″.

White

- Cut 3 strips 12½″ × WOF. Subcut into 8 Template A 12″ pieces.

- Cut 1 strip 3½″ × WOF. Subcut into 10 squares Template A 3″ pieces.

- Cut 5 strips 2″ × WOF. Subcut into 2 strips 2″ × 39½″, 2 strips 2″ × 30½″, 2 strips 2″ × 27½″, 1 strip 2″ × 12½″, 1 strip 2″ × 12″, and 2 strips 2″ × 11¾″.

Red

- Cut 2 strips 6½″ × WOF. Subcut into 8 Template A 6″ pieces.

- Cut 1 strip 1½″ × WOF. Subcut into 10 Template A 1½″ pieces.

CONSTRUCTION

<u>SEAM ALLOWANCE</u> Sew all curved seams with a scant ¼″ seam allowance. Sew all straight seams with an accurate ¼″ seam allowance. Press all straight seams open. Curved seams may be pressed open or toward the center of each circle, toward the Template A (convex) piece.

Creating Arcs

1. Make 2 nested curves units using the technique in Cutting Arcs with Templates (page 15). Make 8 units in sizes 12″/6″ and 10 units in sizes 3″/1½″.

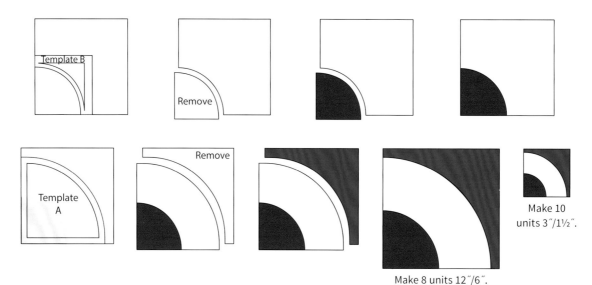

Make 10 units 3″/1½″.

Make 8 units 12″/6″.

2. Join 2 of the 12″/6″ units to make a half circle. Make 4.

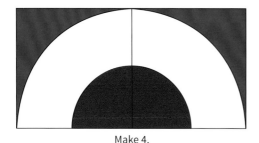

Make 4.

3. Join 2 of the 3″/1½″ units to make a half circle. Make 5.

Make 5.

Assembling the Sections

4. Make the top section as shown in Fig. 1.

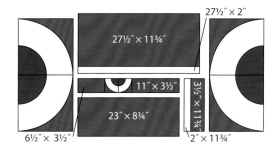

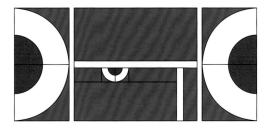

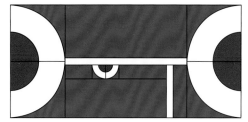

Figure 1

5. Make the middle section as shown in Fig. 2.

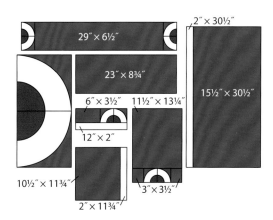

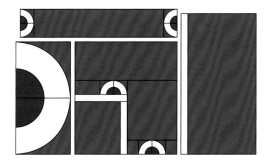

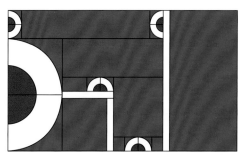

Figure 2

6. Make the bottom section as shown in Fig. 3.

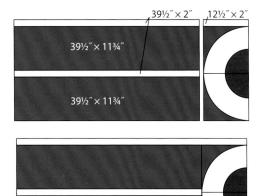

Figure 3

7. Join the 3 sections as shown.

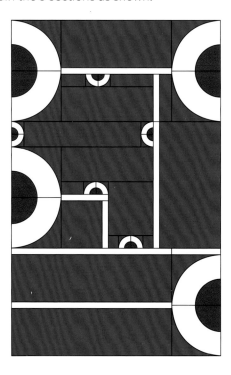

8. Quilt and bind.

GINKGO FANS

Finished quilt: 72″ × 96″

These fans include a variety of shades of three main colors. The yardage amounts listed are the minimum required of each color in order to make the quilt, and the cutting instructions are for yardage that is approximately 41″ from selvedge to selvedge. If you'd like to make the quilt with just three colors, these are sufficient. If you'd like to make a scrappy quilt like the one shown in the picture, gather fat quarters and other scraps from your studio that total a little more than the requirement, and be prepared to get more when needed. In my version, I took the time to match up the background fabrics of the fan so that the color was consistent. You could also go with an easier, completely scrappy approach for a similar look.

I collected the fabrics in this project over a span of ten years, and the resulting quilt is very much like an album for me. Blues and pinks are regularly featured in my quilt designs, so I had an extensive stash of leftovers to work with.

Photo by Øystein Thorvaldsen

Materials

Blue: 4½ yards

Pink: 4½ yards

White: 4½ yards

Binding: ¾ yard

Backing: 6 yards

Batting: 80″ × 104″

TEMPLATES

3″ A (convex), page 128

3″ B (concave), page 128

6″ A (convex), page 125

6″ B (concave), page 124

Cutting

Blue

- Cut 11 strips 3½″ × WOF. Subcut into 128 Template A 3″ pieces.

- Cut 19 strips 3¾″ × WOF. Subcut into 128 Template B 3″ pieces and 64 rectangles 3¾″ × 6¾″. These rectangles are oversize for trimming.

- Cut 6 strips 6¾″ × WOF. Subcut into 64 Template B 6″ pieces.

Pink

- Cut 11 strips 3½″ × WOF. Subcut into 128 Template A 3″ pieces.

- Cut 19 strips 3¾″ × WOF. Subcut into 128 Template B 3″ pieces and 64 rectangles 3¾″ × 6¾″. These rectangles are oversize for trimming.

- Cut 6 strips 6¾″ × WOF. Subcut into 64 Template B 6″ pieces.

White

- Cut 11 strips 3½″ × WOF. Subcut into 128 Template A 3″ pieces.

- Cut 19 strips 3¾″ × WOF. Subcut into 128 Template B 3″ pieces and 64 rectangles 3¾″ × 6¾″. These rectangles are oversize for trimming.

- Cut 6 strips 6¾″ × WOF. Subcut into 64 Template B 6″ pieces.

CONSTRUCTION

SEAM ALLOWANCE Sew all curved seams with a scant ¼″ seam allowance. Sew all straight seams with an accurate ¼″ seam allowance. Press all straight seams open. Curved seams may be pressed open or toward the center of each circle, toward the Template A (convex) piece.

Sew Quarter-Circle Squares

1. Sew all 3″ Template A pieces to 3″ Template B pieces using the technique in Sewing Quarter-Circle Squares (page 20). Make *64 of each* of the following quarter circle units (Template A/Template B):

- blue/white
- blue/pink
- white/pink
- white/blue
- pink/blue
- pink/white

Make 64.

Make 64.

Make 64.

Make 64.

Make 64.

Make 64.

Fan Assembly

2. Sew 2 coordinating quarter circle squares together to make one half of the fan as shown in the illustration. Press.

3. Add a coordinating rectangle to the quarter circle square unit. Press.

4. Trim the unit with the 6″ Template A, ensuring the template is oriented with the straight edge next to the fan curve.

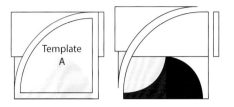

5. Add a coordinating 6″ Template B piece to the fan unit. Trim to 6½″ square, ensuring the ends of the curved seam are ¼″ from the edge of the block. Make 32.

Left fan assembly—make 32.

6. Repeat Steps 2–5 to make 32 right fans.

 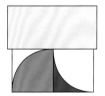 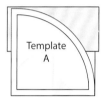

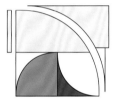 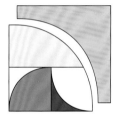 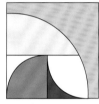

Right fan assembly— make 32.

Double Fans and Assembly

7. Join 4 color-coordinated half fan blocks (2 are mirrored) to create a double fan block. Make 48 blocks of each color composition for a total of 48 blocks.

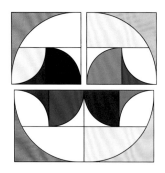
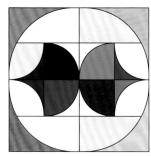

Make 16.

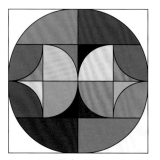

Make 16.

Make 16.

8. Arrange 48 double fan blocks randomly while ensuring an even distribution of each color into 6 rows of 8 blocks each.

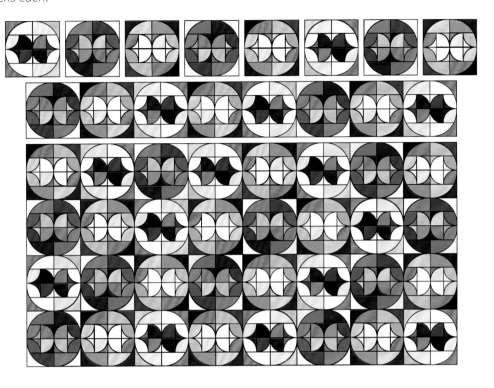

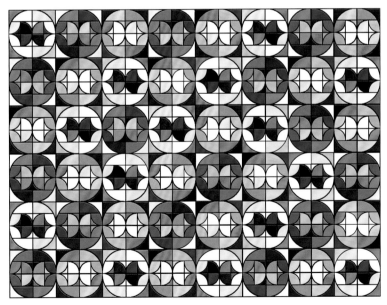

9. Quilt and bind.

CIDER PRESS

Finished quilt: 72″ × 90″

When I was little, my parents sometimes stopped at an apple orchard in the curve of the road on the way home from my grandparents' house in Alabama. We'd walk around and load up on baskets of apples and plastic gallon jugs of cider. Later, when I made a home in Montana, I made apple butter from trays of B grade apples from local orchards each October. These images define the season of autumn for me: ripe red apples; hot mugs of cider. Since we've lived in Norway, I haven't found cider like I'm used to, and I channeled that longing into this quilt.

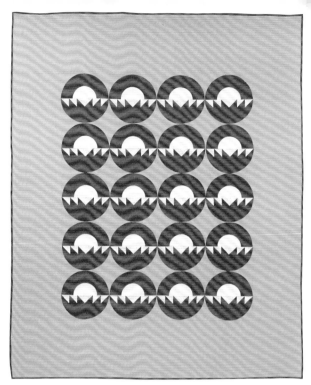

Photo by Alva Thylén

Materials

Red: 3 yards

Peach: ½ yard

Peach print: ½ yard

Brown: 5 yards

Binding: ⅝ yard

Backing: 5½ yards

Batting: 80″ × 98″

FABRIC SELECTION

There are a variety of easy adjustments that can be made to alter the design effects or the speed of the project. I used a solid in the upper center portion of each "apple" and a polka dot print in the half-square triangles to reflect the idea of cider being pressed from the fruit. If the yardage is already in your stash, use the same fabric in the center of the apples as is in the half square triangles. Or to make the project come together a little faster, you can skip the half square triangles and substitute solid material in the bottom of each of the apples.

TEMPLATES

3″ A (convex), page 128

3″ B (concave), page 128

6″ A (covenx), page 125

6″ B (concave), page 124

MATERIAL NOTES

- *Ice Peach Dots by Elizabeth Hartman, Essex Speckle in Mocha, and Kona Solids in Cardinal and Light Parfait from Robert Kaufman Fabrics.*

- *Thread from Aurifil.*

Cutting

Red

- Cut 4 strips 2¾″ × WOF. Subcut into 60 squares 2¾″ × 2¾″.

- Cut 7 strips 4¾″ × WOF. Subcut into 40 rectangles 4¾″ × 6¾″.

- Cut 8 strips 6¾″ × WOF. Subcut into 40 arcs (6″/3″ Arc Template). (It may be more efficient to cut the arcs from continuous yardage without using strips.)

Peach

- Cut 4 strips 3½″ × WOF. Subcut into 40 Template A 3″ pieces.

Peach print

- Cut 5 strips 2¾″ × WOF. Subcut into 60 squares 2¾″ × 2¾″.

Brown

- Cut 8 strips 6¾″ × WOF. Subcut into 80 Template B 6″ pieces.

- Cut 4 strips 15½″ × WOF. Piece for length and subcut into 2 top/bottom borders 15½″ × 72½″.

- Cut 4 strips 12½″ × WOF. Piece for length and subcut into 2 side borders 12½″ × 60½″.

CONSTRUCTION

SEAM ALLOWANCE Sew all curved seams with a scant ¼″ seam allowance. Sew all straight seams with an accurate ¼″ seam allowance. Press all straight seams open. Curved seams may be pressed open or toward the center of each circle, toward the Template A (convex) piece.

Half-Square Triangles

1. Draw a diagonal line on the back of all peach print 2¾″ squares. Place a peach print square and a red square right sides together. Sew a seam ¼″ on either side of the diagonal line. Cut along the drawn line to make 2 half square triangles (HSTs). Press seams open. Trim to 2½″. Make 120 HSTs.

Make 120.

2. Join 3 HSTs together with the red triangles in the bottom left and peach print triangles in the top right. Make 20 units.

Make 20.

3. Join 3 HSTs together with the red triangles in bottom right and peach print triangles in the top left. Make 20 units.

Make 20.

4. Add a red 4¾″ × 6¾″ rectangle to the red side HST. The red rectangle is oversize for efficient sewing and for accurate trimming.

5. Place the 6″ Template B on the pieced square with the straight edge of the template aligned with the peach print along the top edge. Trim the corner.

Template A

6. Mark the center of the curve, and add a brown 6″ Template B piece to the unit. Trim to 6½″. Make 20 left units.

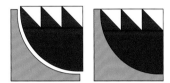

7. Repeat to make 20 right units, as shown.

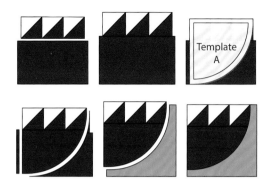

8. Make a nested curves unit with 6″/3″ curves using the technique in Cutting Arcs with Templates (page 15) in brown, red, and peach. Make 40 nested quarter circle square units.

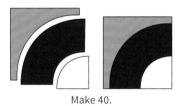

Make 40.

9. Join 2 nested quarter circle square units to make 1 nested half circle unit. Join 2 HST units to make another half circle unit. Join both half circle units to make a full circle. Make 20 full circles.

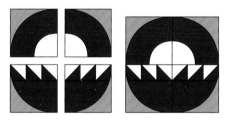

10. Join the blocks into 4 rows of 5 blocks each.

11. Piece the borders as shown in Fig. 1. Add the side borders, and then add the top and bottom borders.

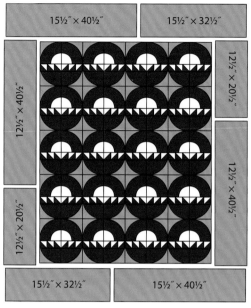
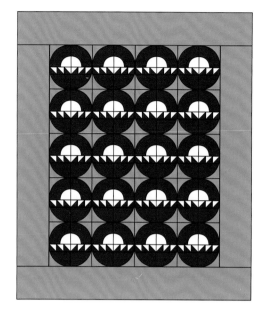

Figure 1

12. Quilt and bind.

Photos by Alva Thylén

LADYBIRD CURVE

Finished quilt: 72″ × 90″

Ladybird Curve began as an exploration of the compass or cardinal directions. After settling on a design that pleased me, I searched for traditional blocks that most resembled the shapes in my arrangement. Traditional motifs often weave their way into my quilt designs, and even if I don't look at them at the beginning of my process, I often like to see how what I've made fits into the larger canon of block designs. The two blocks that seem closest are called Lady of the Lake and Birds in the Air. Without much else of a story to add to the design, I've decided to merge the names of those two traditional blocks and acknowledge the addition of the curve that I love so much.

Materials

Light blue: 1½ yards

Medium blue: 1½ yards

Peach: ¾ yard

Navy: 5 yards

Binding: ⅝ yards

Backing: 5½ yards

Batting: 80″ × 98″

TEMPLATES

6″ A (convex), page 125

6″ B (concave), page 124

MATERIAL NOTES

- *Linear Blocks in Navy and Studio Scissors in Ice Peach from Kept by Carolyn Friedlander, Essex in Sky, and Kona Solid in Fog from Robert Kaufman Fabrics.*

- *Thread from Aurifil.*

Cutting

Light blue

- Cut 8 strips 2¾″ × WOF. Subcut into 100 squares 2¾″ × 2¾″.

- Cut 5 strips 4½″ × WOF. Subcut into 40 squares 4½″ × 4½″.

Medium blue

- Cut 8 strips 2¾″ × WOF. Subcut into 100 squares 2¾″ × 2¾″.

- Cut 5 strips 4½″ × WOF. Subcut into 40 squares 4½″ × 4½″.

Peach

- Cut 8 strips 2¾″ × WOF. Subcut into 100 squares 2¾″ × 2¾″.

Navy

- Cut 8 strips 2¾″ × WOF. Subcut into 100 squares 2¾″ × 2¾″.

- Cut 3 strips 13″ × WOF. Piece for length and subcut into 2 side borders 13″ × 60½″.

- Cut 4 strips 15½″ × WOF. Piece for length and subcut into 2 top/bottom borders 15½″ × 73½″.

- Cut 10 strips 6¾″ × WOF. Subcut into 80 Template B pieces.

ALTERNATE DESIGN IDEAS *The word "ladybird" often refers to the insect commonly called "ladybug." Even though the name for this quilt emerged from a study of existing traditional blocks, substitute a black and red color palette to create your own little ecosystem of ladybugs on a grid. Or combine the fabric requirements for the light blue and medium blue fabrics to make a more unified palette of your own choosing.*

Photo by Alva Thylén

CONSTRUCTION

SEAM ALLOWANCE Sew all curved seams with a scant ¼″ seam allowance. Sew all straight seams with an accurate ¼″ seam allowance. Press all straight seams open. Curved seams may be pressed open or toward the center of each circle, toward the Template A (convex) piece.

Half-Square Triangles

1. Draw a diagonal line on the back of all medium blue 2¾″ squares. Place a light blue square and a navy square right sides together. Sew a seam ¼″ on either side of the diagonal line. Cut along the drawn line to make 2 half square triangles (HSTs). Press seams open. Trim to 2½″. Make 100 light blue/navy and 100 medium blue / peach HSTs.

Make 100.   Make 40.

2. Join 3 blue/peach HSTs horizontally and 2 HSTs vertically with the blue triangles in the top left.

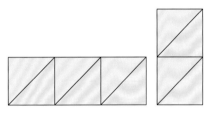

3. Add a light blue 4½″ square to the light blue side of the vertical light blue/navy HST units. Then add the horizontal HST units to the bottom of the square/vertical HST units.

4. Place the 6″ Template A on top of a light blue/navy HST unit so that all HSTs are underneath the template. Trim. Sew a navy 6″ Template B piece to the HST Template A piece. Press and trim to 6½″ × 6½″. Make 40 light blue/navy squares.

 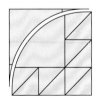  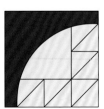

5. Repeat Steps 2–4 to make 40 medium light blue/navy squares.

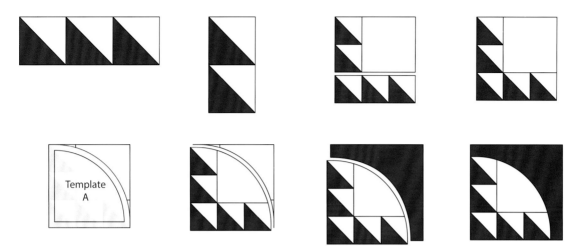

Assemble

6. Join 4 squares (2 of each color) to make a full circle block as shown. Make 20.

7. Join the blocks together into 5 rows of 4 blocks each, orienting the blocks in the same direction.

Make 20.

8. Piece and join the side borders as shown in Fig. 1. Then piece and add the top and bottom borders.

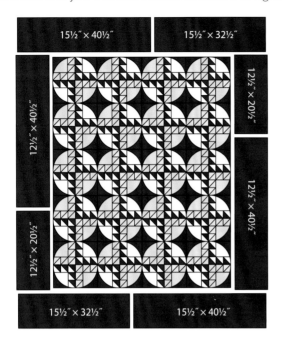

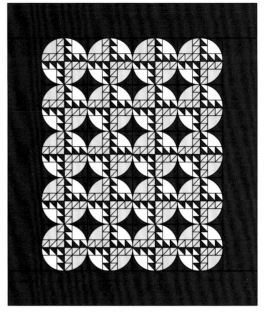

Figure 1

Photo by Alva Thylén

9. Quilt and bind.

Photo by Alva Thylén

SPINNING TRADITION

Finished quilt: 90″ × 90″

The design works well with the blue fabrics arranged in a variety of ways. Feel free to create your own color guide for the block and repeat it throughout the quilt. Or arrange the blue fabrics in different places in each block so that the overall result is truly random. There are 720 curves to be sewn in this quilt, so the key to success is finding a strategy that works for you—and then sew, sew, sew!

Photos by Alva Thylén

Materials

Blue 1: 2¼ yards

Blue 2: ¾ yard

Blue 3: ¾ yard

Blue 4: ½ yard

Blue 5: ½ yard

Blue 6: ¾ yard

Yellow: 1⅜ yard

Light blue: 4 yards

Slate blue: 4½ yards

Binding: ⅔ yard

Backing: 8½ yards

Batting: 98″ × 98″

TEMPLATES

3″ A (convex), page 128

3″ B (concave), page 128

12″ A (convex), pages 124–127

12″ B (concave), page 124–126

MATERIAL NOTES

- *Kept in Navy and Blue, Collection CF in Navy, Blue, Regatta, and Royal by Carolyn Friedlander, Essex Linen in Sky, and Kona Solids in Banana Pepper and Fog from Robert Kaufman Fabrics.*

- *Pieced with 50-weight cotton thread (color 2021) and quilted with Forty3 cotton thread (color 2021) thread from Aurifil.*

- *Numbers next to the blue fabrics match the number in the diagram.*

- *Yardage requirements are exact. If extra material is preferred, add ½ yard to slate blue and ⅛ yard to all remaining colors.*

Cutting

Blue 1

- Cut 21 strips 3½″ × WOF. Subcut into 252 Template A 3″ pieces.

Blue 2

- Cut 6 strips 3½″ × WOF. Subcut into 72 Template A 3″ pieces.

Blue 3

- Cut 6 strips 3½″ × WOF. Subcut into 72 Template A 3″ pieces.

Blue 4

- Cut 3 strips 3½″ × WOF. Subcut into 36 Template A 3″ pieces.

Blue 5

- Cut 3 strips 3½″ × WOF. Subcut into 36 Template A 3″ pieces.

Blue 6

- Cut 6 strips 3½″ × WOF. Subcut into 72 Template A 3″ pieces.

Yellow

- Cut 12 strips 3½″ × WOF. Subcut into 144 Template A 3″ pieces.

Light blue

- Cut 25 strips 3¾″ × WOF. Subcut into 396 Template B 3″ pieces.
- Cut 6 strips 6½″ × WOF. Subcut into 72 rectangles 6½″ × 3½″.

Slate blue

- Cut 3 strips 3½″ × WOF. Subcut into 36 squares 3½″ × 3½″.
- Cut 18 strips 3¾″ × WOF. Subcut into 288 Template B 3″ pieces.
- Cut 6 strips 12¾″ × WOF. Subcut into 36 Template B 12″ pieces.

CONSTRUCTION

SEAM ALLOWANCE Sew all curved seams with a scant ¼″ seam allowance. Sew all straight seams with an accurate ¼″ seam allowance. Press all straight seams open. Curved seams may be pressed open or toward the center of each circle, toward the Template A (convex) piece.

Sew Quarter-Circle Squares

1. Sew all 3″ Template A pieces to 3″ Template B pieces using the technique in Sewing Quarter-Circle Squares (page 20).

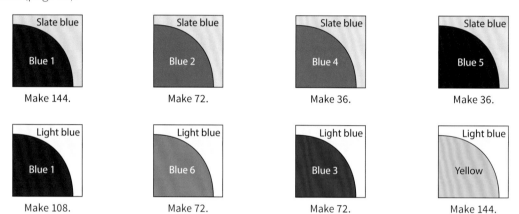

Make a Block Quadrant

2. Join 4 yellow quarter circle squares as shown. Add 2 light blue rectangles.

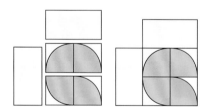

3. Join 4 light blue background quarter circle square units with blue fabrics 3, 1, 6, and 1 in a row as shown.

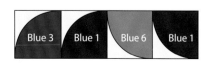

4. Join 3 more light blue background quarter circle square units with blue fabrics 1, 6, and 3 in a row as shown.

5. Add the rows to the yellow unit as shown. Trim the top left corner using the 12″ Template A. Join the slate blue 12″ Template B piece.

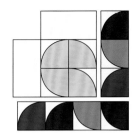 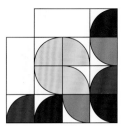 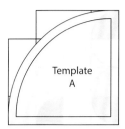

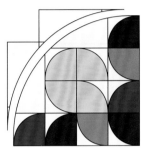 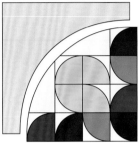 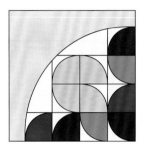

6. Join 4 slate blue quarter circle square units with blue fabrics 1, 4, 1, and 2.

Photo by Alva Thylén

7. Join 4 more slate blue quarter circle square units with blue fabrics 2, 1, 5, and 1, plus a slate blue square.

8. Add the rows to the unit as shown. Make 36.

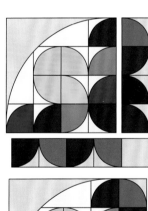

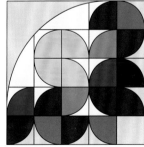

Make 38.

9. Join 4 quadrants to make a block as shown. Make 9 blocks.

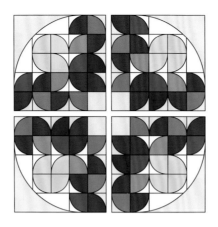

Make 9.

10. Join the blocks into 3 rows of 3 blocks. Then join the rows as shown.

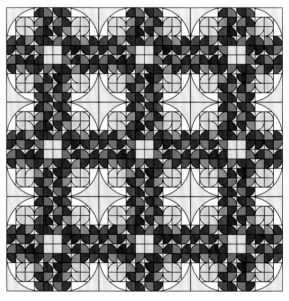

Photo by Alva Thylén

11. Quilt and bind.

Templates

If you prefer to access the nonoverlapping templates digitally, scan this QR code or visit **tinyurl.com/11544-patterns-download** to download the templates.

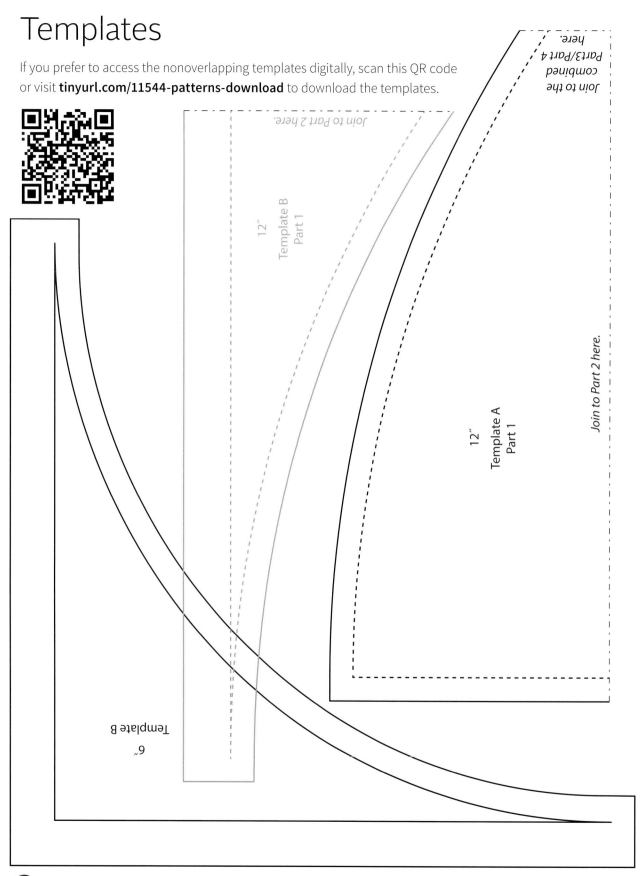

12"
Template B
Part 1

Join to Part 2 here.

12"
Template A
Part 1

Join to the combined Part3/Part 4 here.

Join to Part 2 here.

Template B

6"

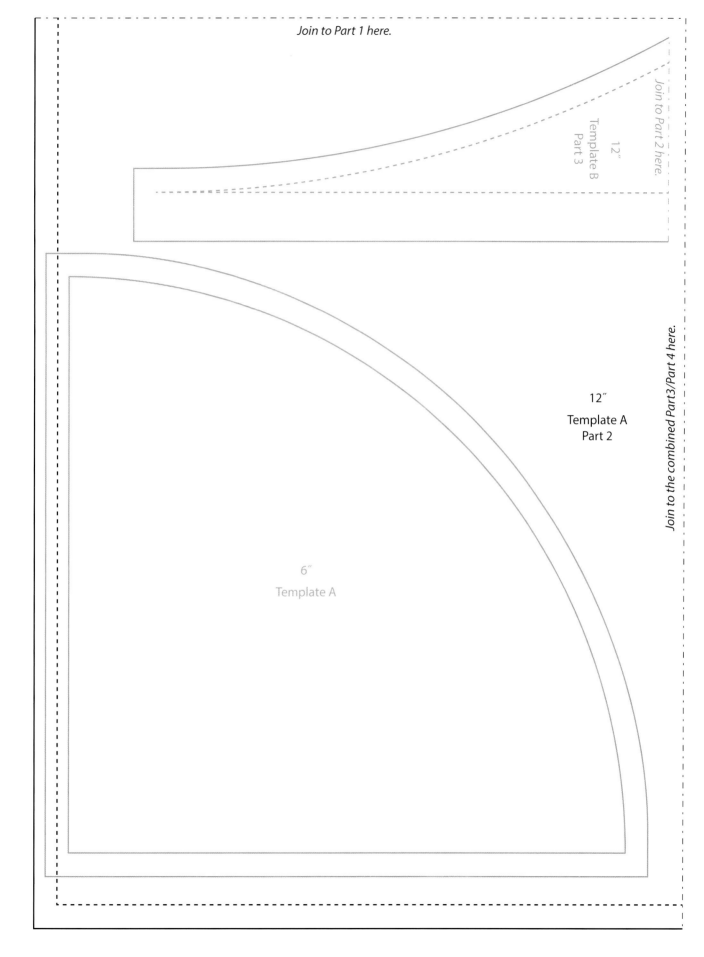

Join to Part 1 here.

Join to Part 2 here.

12″
Template B
Part 3

Join to the combined Part3/Part 4 here.

12″

Template A
Part 2

6″

Template A

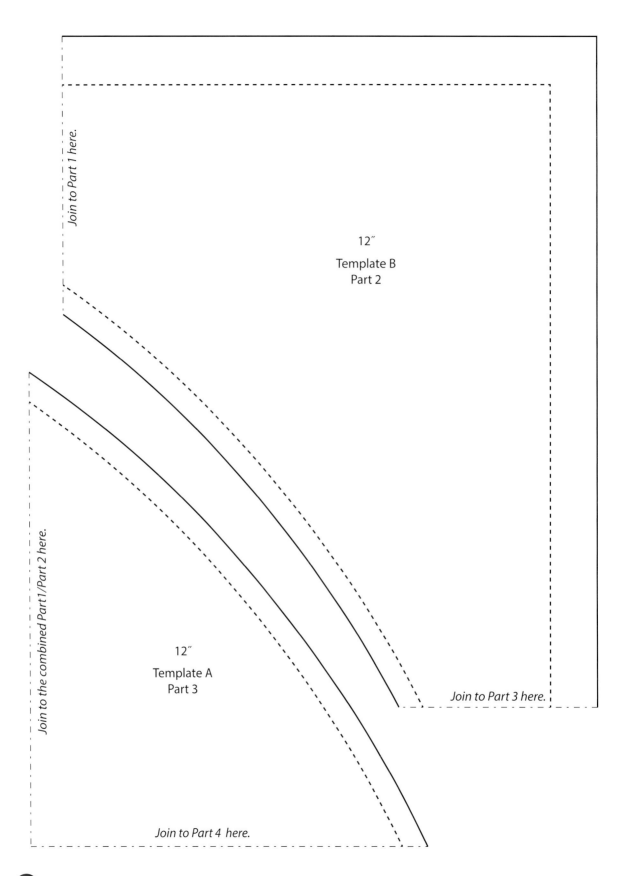

Join to Part 1 here.

12″

Template B
Part 2

Join to the combined Part1/Part 2 here.

12″

Template A
Part 3

Join to Part 3 here.

Join to Part 4 here.

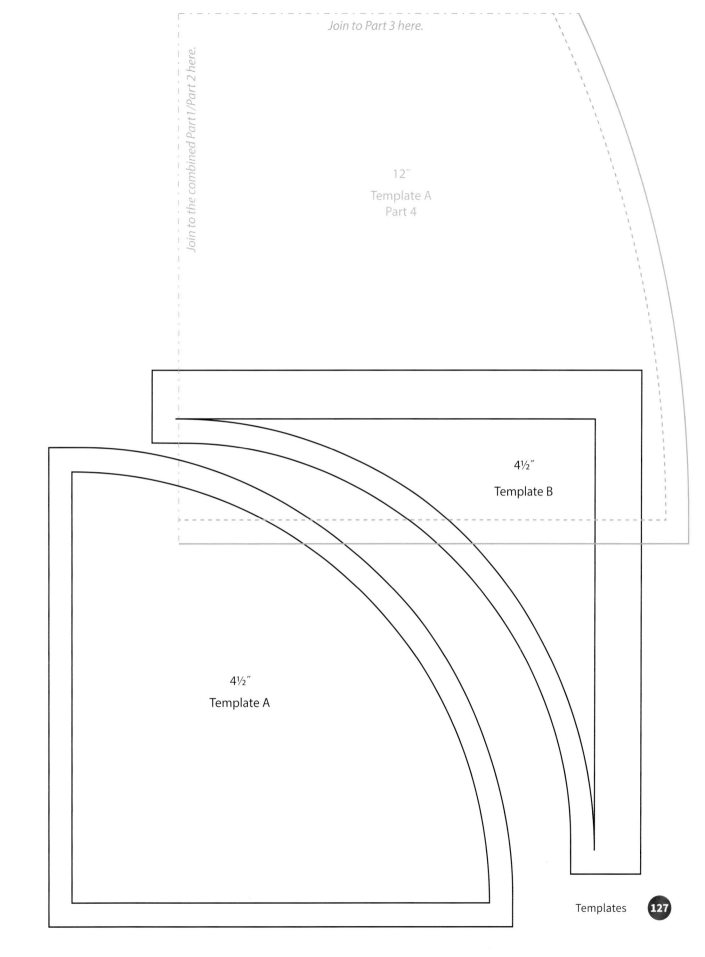

Join to Part 3 here.

Join to the combined Part1/Part 2 here.

12″
Template A
Part 4

4½″
Template B

4½″
Template A

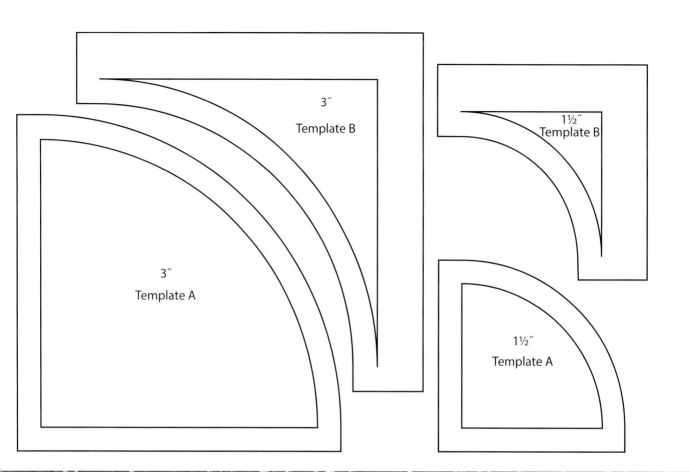

3″
Template B

1½″
Template B

3″
Template A

1½″
Template A

About the Author

Daisy Aschehoug started quilting in 2010 and designing quilts for magazines in 2016. Most of her quilt designs incorporate elements of curved piecing into a modern traditional design aesthetic, and many of her quilt designs have won awards. In 2020, Daisy published her first book with co-author Heather Black: *Quilt Modern Curves and Bold Stripes*. Daisy is a member of Norsk Quilteforbund, the Modern Quilt Guild, and the Studio Art Quilt Associates. Daisy moved to Norway with her family in 2017, and she maintains a quilt studio just south of Oslo in Nesodden.

Visit Daisy online and follow on social media!
Website: warmfolk.com
Instagram: @warmfolk